MASSACRE of the CONESTOGAS

MASSACRE of the CONESTOGAS

On the Trail of the Paxton Boys in Lancaster County

JACK BRUBAKER

THE History PRESS

Published by The History Press
Charleston, SC 29403
www.historypress.net

First published 2010
Second printing 2011
Third printing 2011
Fourth printing 2013

Manufactured in the United States

ISBN 978.1.60949.061.4

Library of Congress Cataloging-in-Publication Data

Brubaker, John H.
Massacre of the Conestogas : on the trail of the Paxton Boys in Lancaster County / Jack Brubaker.
p. cm.
Includes bibliographical references and index.
ISBN 978-1-60949-061-4
1. Paxton Boys. 2. Conestoga Indians--Pennsylvania--Lancaster County--History--18th century. 3. Massacres--Pennsylvania--Lancaster County--History--18th century. 4. Lancaster County (Pa.)--History--18th century. 5. Lancaster County (Pa.)--Race relations--History--18th century. 6. Pennsylvania--History--Colonial period, ca. 1600-1775. I. Title.
F152.B85 2010
974.8'02--dc22
2010039382

For Roger Brubaker, who beat the drum.

It has always been observed, that Indians, settled in the Neighbourhood of White People, do not increase, but diminish continually.
—*Benjamin Franklin,* A Narrative of the Late Massacres, in Lancaster County, of a Number of Indians, Friends of this Province, By Persons Unknown. With some Observations on the same, *1764*

The only good Indians I ever saw were dead.
—*General William Henry Sheridan to the Comanche Chief Toch-a-Way, 1869*

Contents

Preface 11

Part 1: Telling the Story

1. "Drive the Heathen Out of the Land" 17
2. "Some Hot Headed Ill Advised Persons" 25
3. "The Same Spirit & Frantic Rage" 41
4. "Persons of Undoubted Probity & Veracity" 51

Part 2: Retelling the Story

5. "I Never Heard One Word of It Till It Was Just Over" 61
6. "A Mighty Noise and Hubbub" 67
7. "Shot—Scalped—Hacked—and Cut to Pieces" 79
8. "One of Those Youthful Ebullitions of Wrath" 87
9. "The Innocent Were Destined to Share the Fate of the Guilty" 97
10. "A Zone of Vicious Racial Violence" 103

Part 3: Killers and Abettors

11. "The Most Respectable of Men" 113
12. "They Had Possession and Would Keep It" 125
13. "Eternal Shame & Reproach" 133

Part 4: Death and Reconciliation

14. "The Remains of the Victims of a Terrible Crime" 149

15. "Slaughter'd, Kill'd and Cut Off a Whole Tribe" 155

16. "Who Was Left to Mourn for These People?" 161

Notes 169

Bibliography 179

Index 185

About the Author 191

Preface

In December 1763, at least four acts of violence erupted in Lancaster, a county of some twenty-six thousand residents on the east side of the Susquehanna River in south-central Pennsylvania. Two of these incidents are recorded in the official papers of the county's Quarter Sessions Court.

On December 10, John and Margaret Wilson and John Edwards "riotously" assaulted Jane Stevenson, apparently in retaliation for a November assault on Jane Carragan by William Stevenson and six other men. On December 20, William Dickey and two other men "did beat, wound and evilly treat" William Stevenson, apparently precipitating the mangling of John Wilson by Stevenson, his son and five other men in February 1764.

All participants in what seems to have been a fierce feud between the Stevenson and Wilson clans pleaded innocent to charges of assault. The court found all guilty and fined each defendant one British shilling and the costs of prosecution—a relatively stiff penalty at a time when law enforcement often ignored "riots" among the laboring classes.

The other known violent acts of December 1763 are not recorded in court documents because the perpetrators were never charged, arrested or tried. They were never even identified. The court system simply ignored them. While the Stevensons and Wilsons paid a modest price for four rounds of fisticuffs, Scots-Irish militiamen known as the Paxton Rangers got away, scot-free, with murder.

On December 14, some fifty of these Rangers from the Paxton area of northern Lancaster County brutally killed six peaceful Indians living on land set aside for them by William Penn at Conestoga Town in southern Lancaster County. On December 27, fifty to one hundred Rangers and fellow riders murdered fourteen more Conestogas who had been moved into Lancaster Borough, seemingly for their protection.

Some Lancastrians deplored these massacres—which effectively wiped out the tribe—but most residents either cared little about the Conestogas' fate or welcomed the slaughter. Most historians haven't cared much about the Conestogas either but have followed the Rangers to their next destination—Philadelphia. There, in February 1764, a much larger group of Rangers (renamed the Paxton Boys) confronted Pennsylvania authorities and warned that they would kill more Indians under the colony's care. Although they did not carry out their threat, the Paxton Boys flirted with provoking a civil war, altered Pennsylvania politics in the short term and, in the long term, helped lay the foundation for the American Revolution.

This book is primarily concerned with what happened in Lancaster. It is the first effort to examine the massacres of December 1763 and the aftermath in detail. It proposes to provide a more complete understanding, not only of the victims and their killers, but also of the local ministers and magistrates who encouraged the killers and who ultimately refused to apprehend them or bring them to trial.

The book is divided into four parts.

Part 1 describes what occurred in the winter of 1763–64. The narrative follows the most likely scenario, choosing from among sometimes conflicting primary sources.

Part 2 examines how the story has been retold by a long parade of writers—from contemporary observers and early Quaker historians to nineteenth-century apologists for the Scots-Irish Rangers to recent academicians who have reconsidered the incident from the Indians' perspective.

Part 3 explores the Rangers and the men who supported them. No one knows the name of any individual who participated in the massacres, but the motivations of the killers are clear, if complex, and they did not act alone.

Part 4 discusses how the Lancaster County community has dealt with the dead Indians over the decades, both literally and figuratively, and how some twenty-first-century Lancastrians have made efforts to reconcile with contemporary Indians.

Incomplete, contradictory and inaccurate descriptions of the events of December 1763 are common. Unwittingly, I parroted some of this incorrect information in early newspaper columns I wrote for the *Lancaster New Era*. I hope this book helps to clarify the record.

For the most part, I have used the term "Indian," rather than "Native American," to designate the Conestogas and members of other native groups. That terminology was used at the time of the massacres and is preferred by many American Indians today.

I did most of the manuscript research for this book at five institutions with the help of informative staff: American Philosophical Society, Ray Goodman; Dauphin County Historical Society, Warren Wirebach; Historical Society of Pennsylvania; Lancaster County Historical Society, Marianne Heckles, Kevin Shue and Heather Tennis; and Pennsylvania Historical and Museum Commission, Linda Ries, Willis Shirk and Louis Waddell.

A number of persons generously shared their specialized knowledge of various aspects of the subject. Most are named in the text. They include Thomas Barton, David Elder, George Franz, Reaves Goehring Jr., David Johnson, Barry Kent, Barry Kornhauser, Noah Kreider Jr., Janet Richards, Leo Shelley, Owen Stephens, Larry Trump and Ron Wix.

Three friends critiqued and improved a late draft of this work. They are David Schuyler, professor of American studies at Franklin & Marshall College; Peter Seibert, an area historian who has lectured for years on the Paxton Boys and currently directs the National Council for History Education; and Leslie Stainton, an editor and writer at the University of Michigan. I have particularly profited from discussions over several years with Stainton, author of the forthcoming *Ghost Walk*, a history and memoir of the Fulton Opera House, site of the second massacre.

Fred Kinsey, professor emeritus of archaeology at Franklin & Marshall College, read the final draft and suggested changes that refined the text. My niece, Jennifer Veser Besse, performed a comprehensive copyedit.

Hannah Cassilly and the staff of The History Press were as resourceful and generous during the production of this book as they were with my book of newspaper columns, *Remembering Lancaster County: Stories from Pennsylvania Dutch Country*, published earlier this year.

Christine Brubaker endured the ups and downs of her spouse's latest writing obsession and, one memorable afternoon, accompanied me on a walk around the perimeter of the Conestogas' final four hundred acres.

Thanks to all who helped make this book possible.

PART 1

Telling the Story

CHAPTER 1

"Drive the Heathen Out of the Land"

The horses stepped gingerly along the rocky, snow-covered path. The long-coated riders gripped their pommels and rode with ease, guiding the horses as if they were extensions of their bodies. They wore no uniforms but carried the calling cards of war: flintlocks, tomahawks, knives. They looked to the path ahead, only occasionally glancing into the trees and underbrush or, through an opening, to the wide Susquehanna.

Early that morning, December 13, 1763, more than fifty of these riders had assembled near John Harris's Ferry, at a place called Paxton in Lancaster County, Pennsylvania.[1] Most were Scots-Irish Presbyterians, and many were members of the Paxton Rangers, a militia unit formed to protect Paxton and its neighboring townships from marauding Indians.

The riders had traveled downriver from Paxton, adding recruits as they passed through the largely Scots-Irish townships of Derry and Donegal. They had ridden close by the Susquehanna on the Paxtang Path, past the turbulent froth at Conewago Falls and around the great resistant rock at Chickies. As a shrouded sun set, the Rangers rode down the ridge to John Wright's Ferry, a small settlement at another important river crossing.[2] Under threat of even wilder weather at the end of a remarkably cold year that had registered frosts in every season, they had traveled nearly thirty miles. It was time to rest.

The Rangers set off in small groups to find lodging. One gang of men, perhaps ruder than the rest, stayed in the home of a German Mennonite farmer. Late in the night, they tossed their host's pewter on a stove and melted it down.

The militiamen slept lightly and rose before dawn. Snow was falling as they reassembled at the ferry and continued their journey downstream. As they rode, the men reviewed recent events. They cursed hostile Indians for murdering frontier settlers, some of them friends, in the small villages and on the farms to the north and west of Paxton. They thought about how pleasant the fertile land and abundant forests would be if only the hostiles would stop coming down the river to assault unsuspecting families.

In late August, unsettled by recent Indian depredations, some of the Rangers had decided to follow the enemy home. They had ridden north to the Susquehanna's West Branch. There a group of Indians painted for war had surprised the militiamen, killing four and wounding six before disappearing into the woods. Demoralized by the ambush, the Rangers had decided to return to Paxton. Along the way, a small group that had become detached from the main body had run into three Indians returning home after trading at Bethlehem. The Indians had posed no threat, but the Rangers had shot them and returned to Paxton with their scalps—their only emblems of success.

Determined to find and fight hostile Indians, the Rangers in October again had ridden up the Susquehanna, this time along the North Branch. There

Pennsylvania 1763

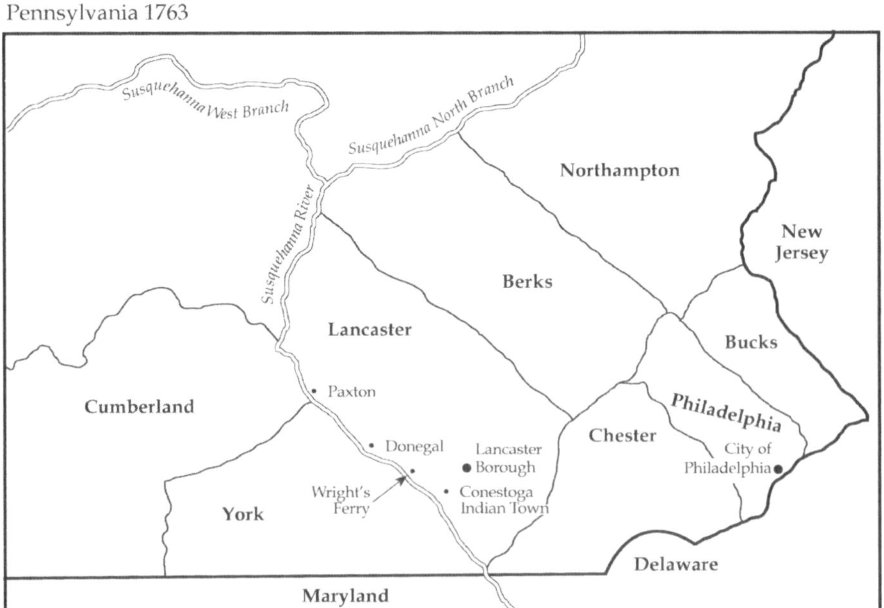

Map by Chris Emlet.

they had found ten members of a Wyoming Valley settlement butchered. The Indians had roasted a woman. They had thrust awls through the eyes of the men. They had run spears and pitchforks through their bodies.

The Rangers again had returned home demoralized. They had little to show for two trips up the river but three scalps, four lost comrades and frightful images of the dead. These images remained fresh on the morning of Wednesday, December 14.

After the riders reached another river-resisting rock, named Turkey Hill after a wild flock, they cut inland along the next ravine carrying a run into the Susquehanna. They rode up the snow-filled ravine to level ground and headed due east toward the Indian village at Conestoga Town. The small cluster of log huts lay near a spring on rising ground some three miles from the river. The people sleeping in the village had no reason to believe that anyone meant to harm them.

For more than seven decades, the Conestogas had enjoyed the protection of Pennsylvania's proprietary government. In 1701, William Penn, founder of the colony, had given the Indians three thousand acres in Manor Township. Sixteen years later, his sons reduced that tract to just over four hundred acres. The Conestogas felt relatively safe in a restricted region

Southern Manor Township 1763

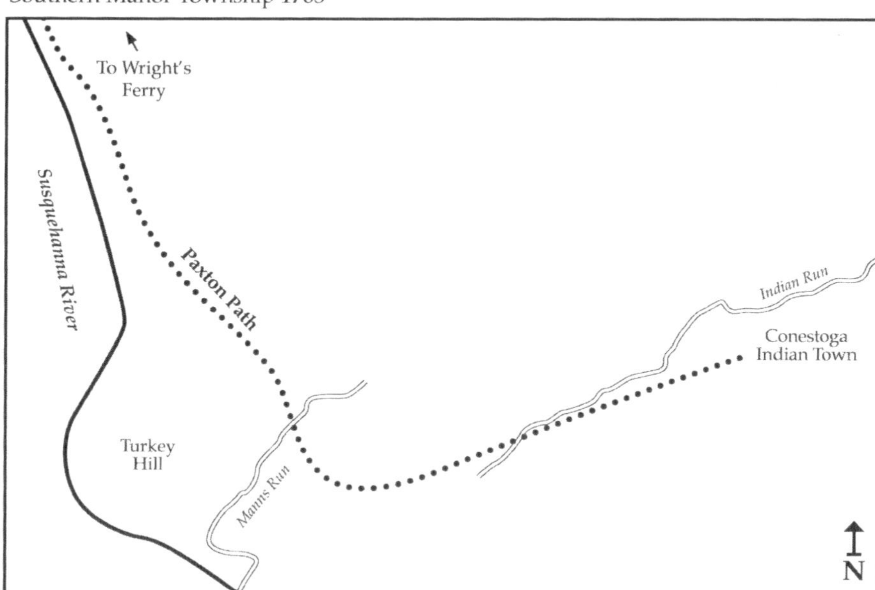

Map by Chris Emlet.

surrounded by sympathetic and pacifistic Mennonite and Quaker farmers. The government had appointed some of these neighbors as caretakers.

As time passed, the Conestogas adopted the customs of many of their neighbors and, increasingly, looked much like them. They abandoned native clothing. They built cabins of wood planks covered with bark. They hunted with imported guns and cooked in iron pots. Many converted to Christianity, at least superficially, after encounters with Catholic missionaries on journeys north to Iroquois country. Although called Conestogas, they actually represented several refugee Indian groups, including Senecas. Most spoke English.

The Conestogas were no longer free roamers. The Mennonites and Quakers had converted most of their old hunting territory into farmland, so the Indians tended vegetable gardens and fished in a nearby stream. They wove brooms and baskets to sell to their neighbors and on the market in the borough of Lancaster, eight miles to the east. When other strategies failed, they went begging, from farm to farm or to Pennsylvania's government in Philadelphia.

Just two weeks before the Paxton Rangers arrived at their camp, the Conestogas petitioned the governor to "consider our distressed situation and grant our women and children some Cloathing to cover them this winter." The Conestogas told the governor that "we are settled at this place by an Agreement of Peace and Amity established between your Grandfather and ours." They said they had been loyal to Pennsylvania throughout the French and Indian War. And they said they remained loyal now, during the latter stages of a postwar "rebellion" directed by the powerful Indian leader Pontiac.

In 1763, only twenty people lived in Indian Town. On December 13, many had traveled several miles from home to peddle their woven wares. Fearing they would be caught outside in a heavy snow if they tried to return, most stayed overnight with a Mennonite farmer and at a nearby ironworks. So on the morning of December 14, only seven people slept in the village.

Many of these sleepers went by two names, their own and those their white neighbors had given them. They were Wa-a-shen, also called George Sock; Tee-Kau-ley, also known as Harry; Kannenquas, a middle-aged woman; Tea-wonsha-i-ong, or Sally, an older woman; her adopted child, Tong-quas, or Chrisly; and Ess-canesh, a young boy. The seventh Conestoga, Ess-canesh's father, was Sheehays or Sohais, often called Old Sheehays, son of Connoodaghtoh. Of the seven, he has the most substantial biography.

Sheehays was so old, some said, that he had met with William Penn at the treaty session that had established Conestoga in 1701. Sheehays had been the tribe's chief in the late 1750s and he had attended treaty sessions

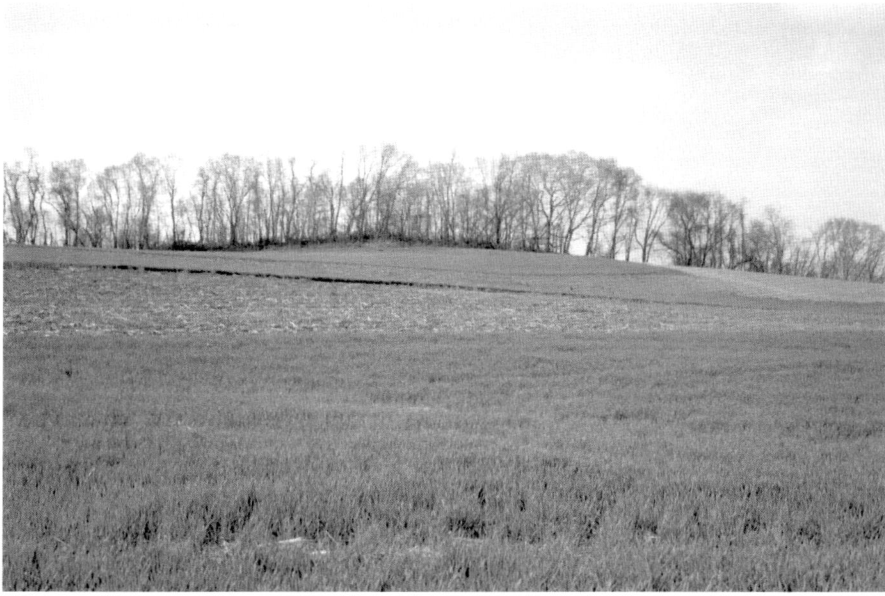

Indian Round Top rises near one of several eighteenth-century locations of Conestoga Indian Town. *Photo by Christine Brubaker.*

for decades. He had signed treaties the way he had signed the letter to the governor asking for winter clothing—by drawing a simple songbird on parchment. Settlers at Wright's Ferry considered Sheehays a great friend. He felt the same about them. When someone had suggested that angry white men someday might come and murder him and his people, Sheehays had scoffed. "It is impossible," he had said. "The English will wrap me in their matchcoat, and secure me from all danger."

The Conestogas slept soundly, unsuspectingly in the continuing snowfall. As slender plumes of smoke rose from their fire-warmed huts, neither Old Sheehays, Ess-canesh nor any other sleeper was eager to beat the sunrise.

First light and the Paxton Rangers arrived together at Conestoga Town. The Rangers went about their business in a rush. They dismounted and fired their flintlocks at the Indian huts. They rushed inside and tomahawked the survivors. They scalped everyone. Then they looted the huts, lashed the booty to their saddles and set the buildings on fire.

The entire operation must have consumed only minutes. The Rangers remounted and, energized by the ease of their slaughter, rode rapidly from the village. It would be a long day's ride back to Paxton. Worried wives would be waiting.

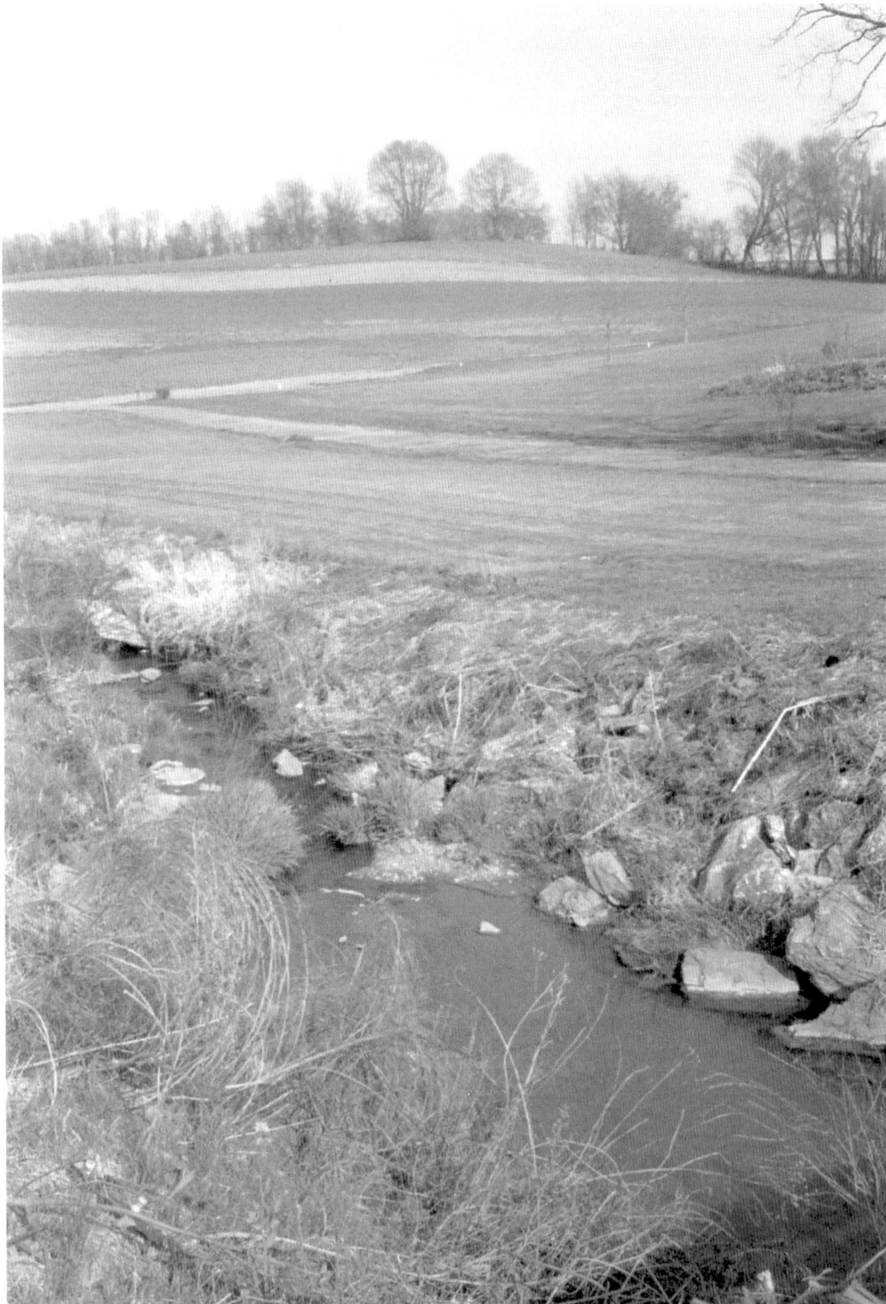

Indian Run flows through the Conestoga Indians' four-hundred-acre tract in Manor Township. *Photo by Christine Brubaker.*

The victorious column had traveled only a couple of miles when it encountered Thomas Wright, one of the Conestogas' Quaker neighbors. Suspecting the Rangers' mission but not knowing it had been accomplished, Wright reminded the riders that Pennsylvania's government protected the Conestogas. The Rangers replied that no government should protect Indians. "Joshua was ordained to drive the heathen out of the land," they said. They asked, "Do you believe the scriptures?" Wright had no ready response, and the Rangers left the peace-professing Quaker standing stunned in the snow.

The killers stopped briefly at Wright's Ferry. They again separated into small groups, one of which went knocking at the oak door of Robert Barber Jr., a Quaker leader in the riverside community. Removing overcoats encrusted with snow, five or six Rangers entered the settlement's oldest brick house to warm themselves by one of its many fireplaces.

In the course of their conversation, the men asked Barber why he and his neighbors allowed Indians to live among them in uncertain times. Barber replied that the Conestogas were peaceful and inoffensive. So the Rangers asked what would happen if someone killed these Indians. Barber said he thought the killers would be as liable to punishment as if the Indians had been white men. The killers said they believed otherwise.

During this discussion, two of Barber's sons walked outside. Tied to the saddles of the raiders' horses they saw bloody tomahawks and young Chrisly's toy gun. The boys had played with Chrisly—he had made bows and arrows for them; they had given him the gun—and the blood on the tomahawks alarmed them.

Soon after the Rangers rode away, Barber's sons described what they had seen. Fearing the worst, Barber and other Wright's Ferry Quakers rapidly rode to Indian Town. They were horrified to discover the burned bodies of the Indians lying amid the ruins of their huts.

Meanwhile, Chrisly had escaped. He alone had heard the Rangers approaching the village and had slipped away to run through the snow to inform Captain Thomas McKee.

McKee, another Conestoga neighbor and caretaker, listened to the story from the breathless boy with frozen feet. Then he sent a messenger to inform Lancaster County's chief magistrate that the Conestogas and their village had been destroyed. Upon receiving the message, Edward Shippen III, chief of all Lancaster County judges, dispatched Matthias Slough, the county coroner, and John Hay, the county sheriff, to Indian Town. Their instructions: discover who had killed the Conestogas.

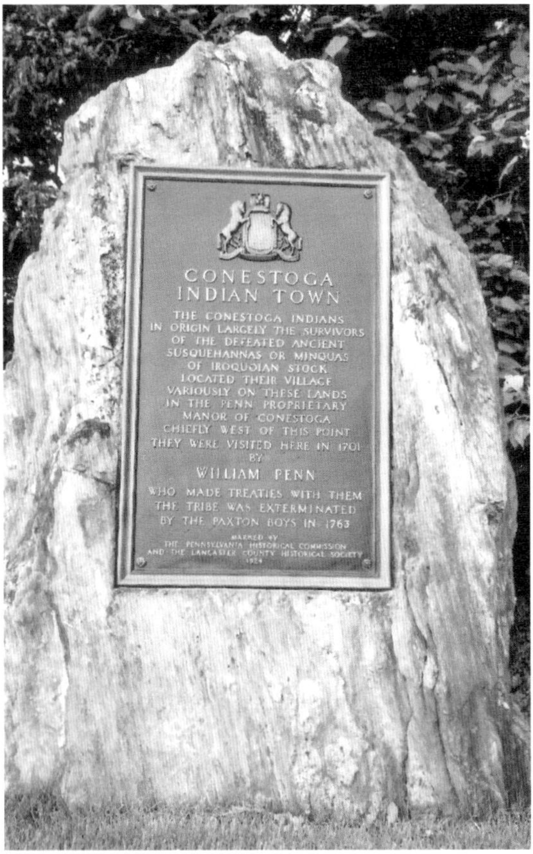

A memorial boulder designates the site of Conestoga Indian Town in Manor Township. *Photo by the author.*

Slough, Hay and thirteen other Lancaster residents dressed for white weather and rode out to Conestoga Town. They found the ravaged village, with all of the huts but one burned entirely to the ground. After poking through the charred remains, finding bodies scattered here and there in the ashes, the somber white men conferred. In the officious jargon of their "Coroners Inquisition," they determined that the Indians had been slaughtered by "a person or persons to this Inquest unknown." Then Slough contributed some money for burial, and the Barber party laid the bodies in the snow-covered ground.

When the remaining Conestogas returned to find a third of their number dead and their village destroyed, they wept and wondered what would become of them. Once again they sought shelter with Mennonite neighbors. There they were surprised and in part consoled to encounter Chrisly and his survivor's story.

CHAPTER 2

"Some Hot Headed Ill Advised Persons"

Most Lancastrians learned about the massacre at Conestoga Town by Thursday, December 15. And by the next day, the provincial government at Philadelphia knew what had happened in the tiny Indian village near the Susquehanna some seventy miles to the west. In Lancaster and in Philadelphia, officials began to worry that the violent men who had murdered and burned the Conestogas might not stop with one assault.

The Paxton militiamen had ample reason to hate Indians. In 1757, at the outset of the French and Indian War, hostile Indians aligned with the French had raided Paxton, killing several inhabitants and burning their homes. The memory of that attack remained vivid among Paxtonians, even as assaults east of the Susquehanna diminished and the fighting shifted westward.

Conflict escalated again in the summer of 1763 as Pontiac, a charismatic Ottawa warrior in the Detroit area, led several groups of Indians in an armed protest against expanding British settlement following the French defeat. The violence overwhelmed forts and killed dozens of settlers as it rippled toward south-central Pennsylvania. For a time, Pontiac's forces threatened to destabilize the entire frontier with the most concentrated Indian attacks the colonists had yet seen.

That summer and autumn, the Paxton Rangers guarded the northernmost section of Lancaster County. Renewed depredations in areas not far from their picket lines, along with their own frightful tours up the Susquehanna, reinforced what the Rangers had decided during the war: all Indians were enemies. They concluded, without substantial evidence, that Pennsylvania's

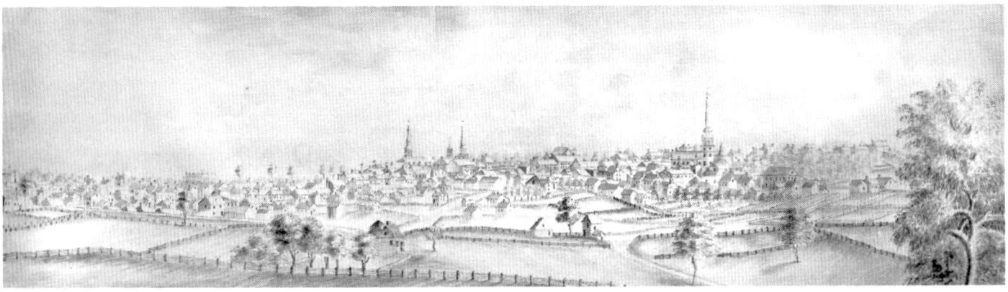

A view of Lancaster from the southwest, about 1800, shows a town that has sprawled east and west from its center since the massacre of 1763. The cupola of the county courthouse rises between church spires at center, and St. James Episcopal Church's spire rises to the immediate right of the courthouse. The county prison is down West King Street hill, just over midway between the courthouse and the left edge of the drawing. *Heritage Center of Lancaster County.*

"friendly" Indians were monitoring white settlements and providing information to hostiles.

The Rangers were concerned about two groups: Lancaster County's Conestogas and a band of Lenni Lenapes in Northampton County. The Lenapes had been converted by German Moravians in Bethlehem and were called Delawares or Moravian Indians in the white settlements. Many Rangers, however, called both the Lenapes and Conestogas spies.

John Elder commanded the Paxton Rangers and ministered to many of them at his church, Paxton Presbyterian. Elder advocated the removal of the Conestogas and Moravian Indians from the volatile frontier to the relative safety of Philadelphia, seat of the provincial government. The minister said he believed the move not only would preserve the Indians from possible frontier vengeance, but it also would limit any opportunity for them to act as spies. John Harris Jr., son of the pioneer ferry operator and the wealthiest landholder in Paxton, also appealed to the governor to move the Indians. He said hostile attacks had poisoned the atmosphere and threatened the safety of Indians living among whites.

The government accepted part of this advice that November and moved the 125 Moravian Indians to Philadelphia. But John Penn, the founder's thirty-three-year-old grandson, who just weeks before had become Pennsylvania's chief political officer, refused to move the Conestogas. Governor Penn believed that the Conestogas, unlike the Moravian Indians, had been taken directly under the government's wing and should be preserved in place. "The faith of this Government is pledged for their protection," he reasoned. "I cannot remove them without adequate cause."

So when Penn learned of the massacre at Conestoga, he claimed the assault was a personal affront against him as an agent of the king. He denounced the killers who "did, without cause or provocation, and in defiance of all Authority...murder Six of our Friendly Indians, settled there under the Protection of this Government and Its Laws." Penn instructed the magistrates of Lancaster, York and Cumberland Counties to issue warrants and apprehend and imprison the killers "that they may be brought to Justice, & receive a legal tryal for the Crimes they have committed."

Colonel John Armstrong, an Irish-born war hero and commandant at Carlisle, Cumberland County, during Pontiac's uprising, replied to Penn. He said the magistrates of Cumberland County would issue warrants. But he claimed that no one from Cumberland County had been involved in the killings "and I should be very sorry that ever the people of this County should attempt avengeing their injuries on the heads of a few inoffensive superannuated Savages, whome nature had already devoted to the dust."

Lancaster County officials also distanced themselves from the massacre. Elder told Penn that he and Justice Thomas Forster, also of Paxton and Elder's parishioner, had pleaded with the Rangers not to kill the Indians on the day before the attack. The two men could not prevail, Elder wrote, against "some hot headed ill advised persons, & especially by such, I imagine, as suffer'd much in their relations by the Ravages committed in the late Indian War." From Lancaster, Justice Edward Shippen wrote to Elder asking why fifty men had ridden all the way from Paxton to kill six Indians under the government's care. But he absolved Elder of personal guilt. "If you had had the least knowledge of such a wicked design," he assured the minister, "you would have done all in your Power to Have Prevented its being carried into Execution."

Shippen expressed some concern that the Rangers might continue their "riotous behavior" and return for the scalps of the remaining Conestogas. He ordered his deputies to move the Indians into a safe building in Lancaster Borough. That building, a substantial brick workhouse, stood directly north of the county jail at King and Prince Streets, just a block down King Street hill from Lancaster's busy Centre Square.

The Pennsylvania Assembly had just authorized this new building in early 1763, so the Conestogas became some of its first inmates. The workhouse, or "House of Correction," was designed not for the most serious lawbreakers, who were confined in the jail, but "for the correcting and keeping at hard labor all rogues, vagabonds, sturdy beggars and idle and dissolute persons." The workhouse, like the jail, was fronted on Prince Street. At its rear, an

Central Lancaster Borough 1763

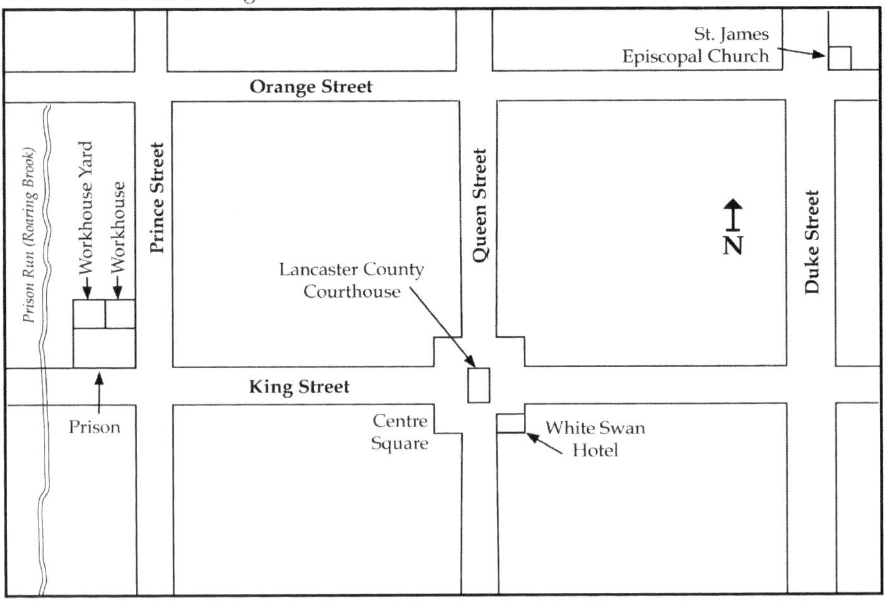

Map by Chris Emlet.

open yard sloped toward a tall stone wall bordering Prison Run, which flowed south to the Conestoga River.[3]

John Hay Jr., the sheriff's son, and Robert Beatty and John Miller, two of the government's overseers at Indian Town, told the fourteen Conestogas to travel to Lancaster. The Indians moved into the workhouse in shifts. Robert Thompson and Dr. Adam Simon Kuhn, two of Shippen's fellow justices, processed the first four on December 16, two days after the massacre at Conestoga. Sheriff Hay brought in the other ten, including young Chrisly, the next day. In a letter to his son in Philadelphia, Shippen explained that the Indians consented to the move "because they know it was for their preservation."

The magistrate quickly added that the move also would preserve the community from the Indians: "Had it not been for the great Snow which fell here the day the Indians were killed at the Conestogo Town, harmless as they might have been before, it would not have been in our Power to have put them under any confinement, but they would immediately have sought revenge."

By the act of moving the Indians into a county facility, Shippen and Lancaster's other magistrates took personal responsibility for their welfare.

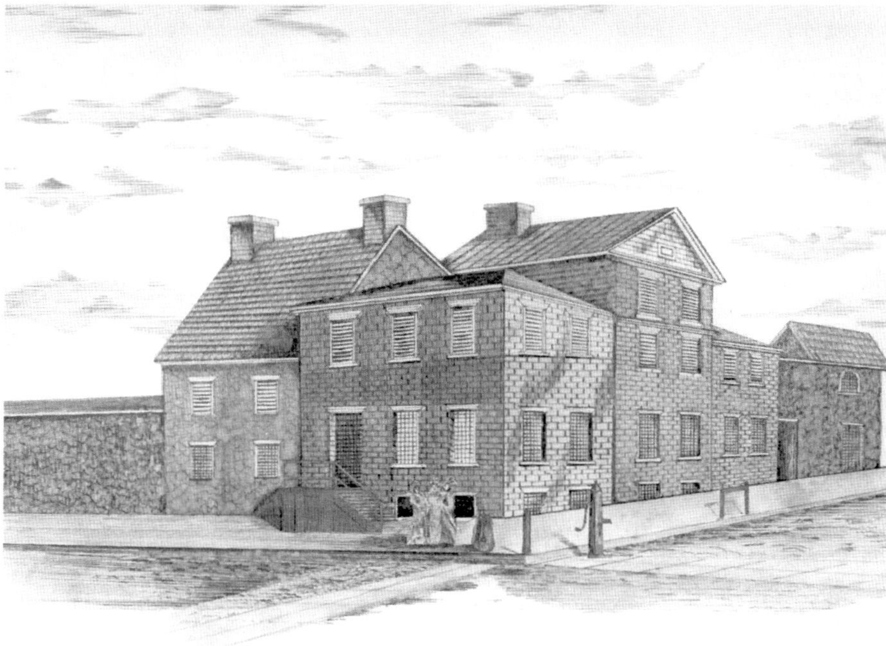

An early depiction of Lancaster County Prison at King and Prince Streets shows the workhouse section, where the Conestogas were housed and killed, at far right. *Lancaster County Historical Society.*

John Penn punctuated that decision on December 21 when he told the Pennsylvania Assembly that the surviving Conestogas "are now taken under the protection of the Magistracy at Lancaster, and are secured in the Workhouse there."

Of the seven adults and seven children who were now wards of both colony and county, the most prominent was Tenseedaagua, also called Toshetaquah. Better known as Will or Bill Sock, Soc or Sack, depending on who was saying and spelling his name, Will was the brother of George Sock who died at Conestoga. Will and George Sock were well known in the county, so when the Paxton Rangers said the Conestogas were fraternizing with and spying for hostile Indians, they primarily meant the Sock brothers.

Will Sock spoke Seneca and English. He participated in treaty sessions, often serving as interpreter, and he helped assemble the only known written vocabulary of the Susquehannocks. Early in the French and Indian War, he traveled with and carried messages for the British army. He frequently visited other Indian villages. He also attempted, unsuccessfully, to persuade the Conestogas to move north to a place with a larger concentration of Indians.

Sock was by far the most worldly of the Conestogas, and reportedly the least submissive, which itself probably invited suspicion. Accounts of Sock's exploits are not hard to find, but many are hearsay. Credible reports about Will Sock in Lancaster's wider community are mixed. Some believed he had "murder in his heart" and, perhaps, on his hands; others insisted he had never "hurt a hair of one head of any Whiteman."

Sock was accompanied by his wife, Kanianguas, or Molly. Kanianguas was Old Sheehays's mourning daughter and a significant member of the tribe. She had served as interpreter during a recent conference between Pennsylvania's government and the Conestogas at Lancaster.

Sheehays's surviving sons, both young boys—Ex-undas and Shae-e-kah, or Jacob—also came to the workhouse.

Kyunqueagoah, or Captain John, was an old man, reported at various times as having accompanied Sock and Sheehays in their travels. His son, Tee-Kau-ley, had been killed at Conestoga. Kyunqueagoah's wife, Koweenasee, or Betty, joined him, along with Hy-ye-naes, or Little Peter, Koweenasee's young son.

Quaachow, or Little John, son of Kyunqueagoah, apparently was an unmarried adult.

Saquies-hat-tah, or John Smith, came to the workhouse with his wife, Chee-na-wan, or Peggy.

Three girls, all described as "little," also entered the workhouse. They were Ko-qoa-e-un-quas, or Molly; Canu-kie-sung, or Peggy; and Karen-do-uah.

Chrisly was the seventh child.

The Conestogas had few possessions besides the clothing they were wearing and the baskets and brooms they were selling when the Rangers burned their town. As he checked the Indians into the workhouse, Sheriff Hay prepared a written inventory of their other belongings: three horses, two belts of wampum (beaded belts used as currency and jewelry) and half a dozen treaties and letters exchanged between them and various Pennsylvania officials.

The oldest of these papers was the treaty forged between the Indians and William Penn and apparently witnessed by Old Sheehays. In that hopeful document, dated April 23, 1701, the Conestogas and Penn had pledged "that they shall forever hereafter be as one Head & One Heart, & live in true Friendship & Amity as one People."

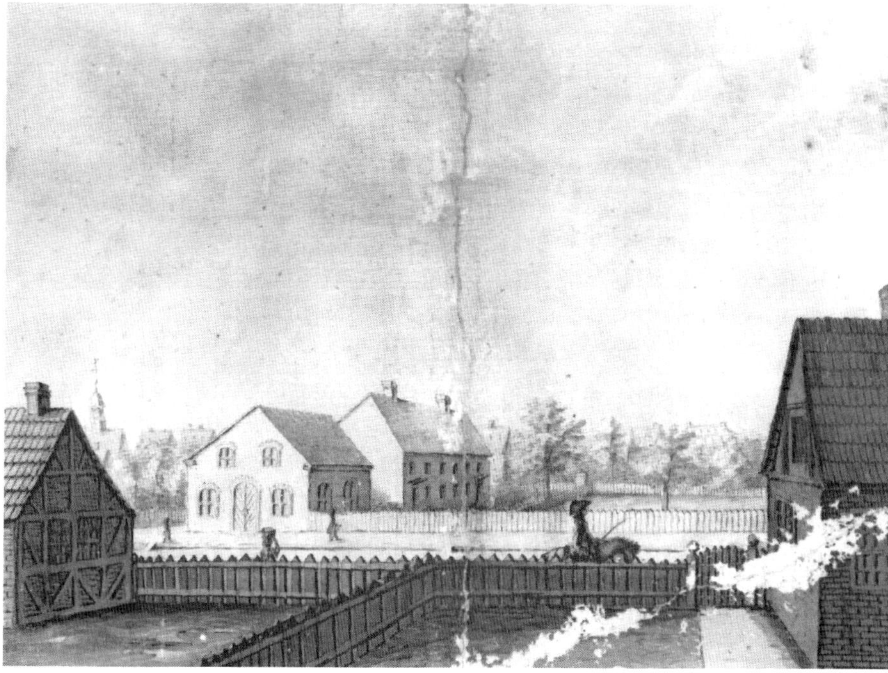

Moravian artist Nicholas Garrison Jr. painted the earliest existing view of Lancaster in 1757, six years before the massacre. The Moravian Church stands at left on West Orange Street. The cupola of the first courthouse in Centre Square rises at far left. *Moravian Archives, Bethlehem.*

Lancaster's weather remained frigid. The snow that had fallen on December 14 did not melt. The Conestogas must have spent most of their time inside the workhouse, huddled against its fireplace. But on sunny afternoons, the adults may have walked out into its rear yard, on paths beaten down to ice, while their young children tumbled in the snow. For people mourning the deaths of relatives and friends, burned out of their homes, imprisoned and living on the welfare of the white community, these days must have seemed endlessly bleak.

Most of the two thousand residents of Lancaster ignored the plight of the Conestogas. A substantial town of more than five hundred houses and significant commerce—one of the largest inland communities in the colonies—was busy with its daily affairs.

That Sunday, December 18, many people assembled at half a dozen churches within a few blocks of the workhouse. On Monday, Shippen and other judges returned to work in the two-story brick county courthouse in the middle of Centre Square. The borough's shopkeepers and wagon makers, bakers and carpenters busied themselves at their trades. Dr. Kuhn resumed his medical practice; William Henry and Joseph Simon manufactured their firearms; and Robert Fulton Sr., father of the future steamboat entrepreneur, toiled in his tailor shop. In the evening, convivial residents passed a few hours

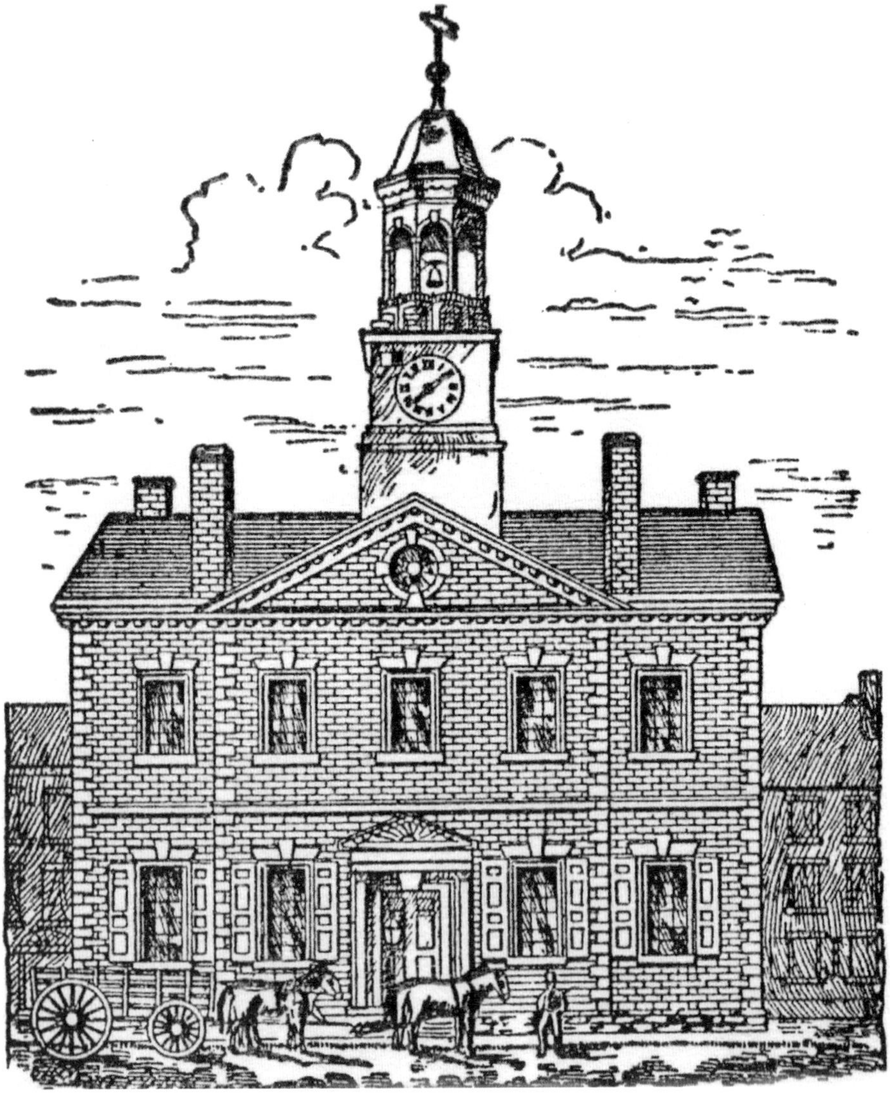

Lancaster County's second courthouse. It essentially replicated the first, which was built in 1739 and burned in 1786. *Lancaster County Historical Society.*

drinking whiskey and rum at Coroner Slough's popular, three-story brick hotel and tavern, the Sign of the White Swan, on the square's southeast corner. Most of Lancaster's prominent visitors stayed at the White Swan, which served not only as the borough's primary social center but also as the Slough family residence.

The Ranger problem forcefully reasserted itself late on December 20. Felix Donnally, keeper of the prison and workhouse, informed Shippen that he had heard that some of the men who had killed the Indians at Conestoga had reassembled. He said the Rangers had been seen in taverns on the Donegal Road, a highway leading to the Presbyterian meetinghouse at Donegal, midway between Lancaster and Paxton. Donnally had heard that other men would join these Rangers before midnight and that the enlarged group would ride into town, break open the workhouse and kill the rest of the Conestogas.

Shippen consulted with James Bickham, Lancaster's chief burgess and a fellow magistrate. The men decided to send two constables to collect information. "If on their Return we found the Story to be true," Shippen later wrote to his son, "we Should immediately alarmn the Borough; and do the best we could to prevent the Indians being killed."

Shippen, Bickham and other magistrates and burgesses waited together for the constables until early on the morning of December 21. Then the scouts returned from the Donegal Road taverns, Shippen reported, "almost perished with the cold and gave us the pleasure to hear that there were no Rioters at either of those places, nor had any of them been seen thereabouts since they came from the Conestogoe Town."

That was sufficient reassurance for borough officials. They decided the report of an imminent attack was unsubstantiated, delegated protection of the Conestogas to Hay and Donnally and went about their business. No one posted armed guards at the workhouse. No one alerted Captain James Robertson, whose regiment of Royal Scottish Highlanders was then staying in homes throughout the borough.

But Donnally, who lived in the jail with his family, believed the threat of attack was serious enough to send his children to live elsewhere. And he and several magistrates were sufficiently worried that they walked up and down Prince Street in front of the workhouse on several cold nights.

At the same time, Penn reported to the assembly that he had just learned that the Conestogas themselves had asked to be moved to Philadelphia for their safety. Abandoning his opposition to the move, Penn said he was willing to make the transfer if lawmakers covered travel expenses. On December

21, the assembly agreed to move the Indians to the capital "as soon as it can conveniently be done."

On December 22, Penn issued a pointed proclamation, underscoring his letter to the magistrates of December 19. Although he offered no reward for the Indian killers, he again denounced them and again charged all judges and other officials with finding and jailing them. Additionally, he forbade anyone to injure the Moravian Indians in Philadelphia.

But Lancastrians paid little attention to Penn's fulminations, focusing not on the fate of the Indians or their adversaries but on the upcoming Christmas celebration. Most of the borough's churches planned to mark the holiday with solemnity and joy.

The traditional Christmas day, which fell on a Sunday, passed peacefully in the borough, and on December 26, everyone but Germans, many of whom celebrated a second day of Christmas, returned to work. December 27 began as a workday for Anglicans, but in the early afternoon, Lancaster's English elite abandoned their labor and made their way to St. James Episcopal Church for a delayed Christmas service.

The Reverend Thomas Barton, St. James's minister, also served as pastor of substantial Anglican congregations in Churchtown and Pequea, villages

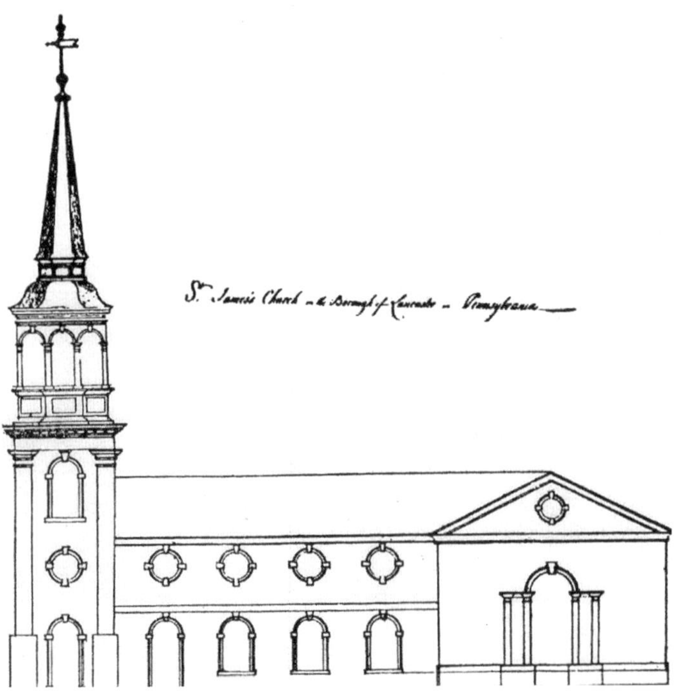

An architect's drawing of St. James Episcopal Church as it appeared in 1762, the year before the massacre. *Lancaster County Historical Society.*

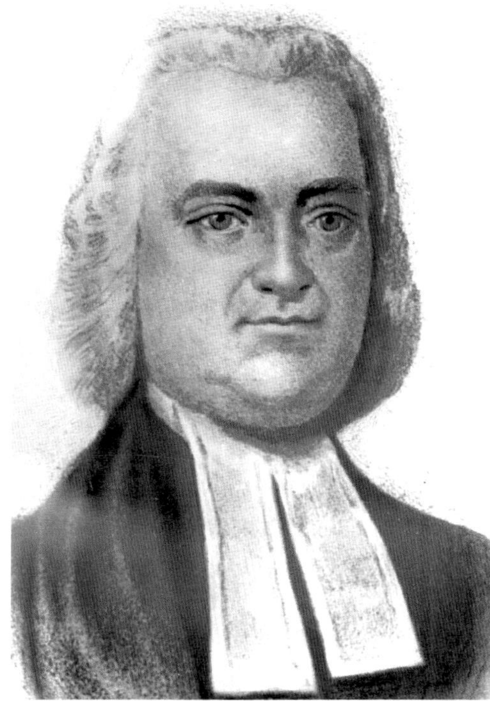

Thomas Barton, rector of St. James Episcopal Church, presided over a delayed Christmas service as the Paxton Rangers killed the Conestogas. *Lancaster County Historical Society.*

elsewhere in Lancaster County. Barton planned the Christmas Day service at Pequea. He would not hold the holiday service in Lancaster until Tuesday, December 27.

Many of Lancaster's leading citizens, including a small but influential gentry, were bound to attend the delayed celebration in the limestone church that had been erected at the corner of Duke and Orange Streets a decade earlier. Beyond serving prominently in public affairs, several of these men were church wardens or vestrymen.

Justice Shippen customarily attended First Presbyterian Church. But Presbyterians, like Quakers, ignored overt celebrations of Christmas, so Shippen would observe the third of the twelve days of Christmas in his secondary pew at St. James. Chief Burgess Bickham would sit nearby. Other prominent Lancaster figures attending the service would include Dr. Kuhn; Dr. Samuel Boude, who eventually would serve in the state legislature; William Henry, the gunsmith who would experiment with steam engines on water before Robert Fulton Jr.; George Ross, who would sign the Declaration of Independence; and William Augustus Atlee, who would become a Pennsylvania Supreme Court justice and chief burgess of Lancaster.

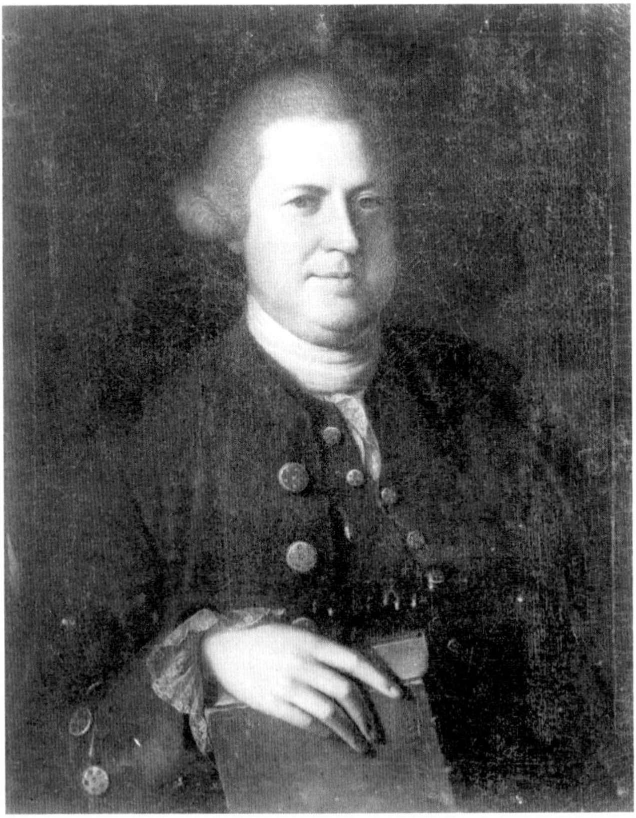

Edward Shippen, chief magistrate of Lancaster County when the Conestogas were massacred. *Historical Society of Pennsylvania.*

At precisely two o'clock that afternoon, Barton, an Irish-born scholar known for crafting powerful sermons, began working his way through the familiar holiday service. The pillars of the community sat comfortably by their wives in the candlelit, evergreen-scented church.

Suddenly, just minutes after the start of the program, agitated messengers threw open the church doors. They cried out that armed and angry men had broken into the community workhouse and were killing the Conestogas. The male parishioners headed for the door. Outside, all was consternation; but by the time Shippen, Bickham and the others had made their way down the hill to the workhouse some three blocks away, the killers had ridden out of town.

Everyone soon knew what had happened. The county's newest public building had been turned into a charnel house. All of the Conestogas were dead. No one had tried to stop the slaughter, and the murderers had ridden out of Lancaster, as one witness reported, "hooping and hallowing."

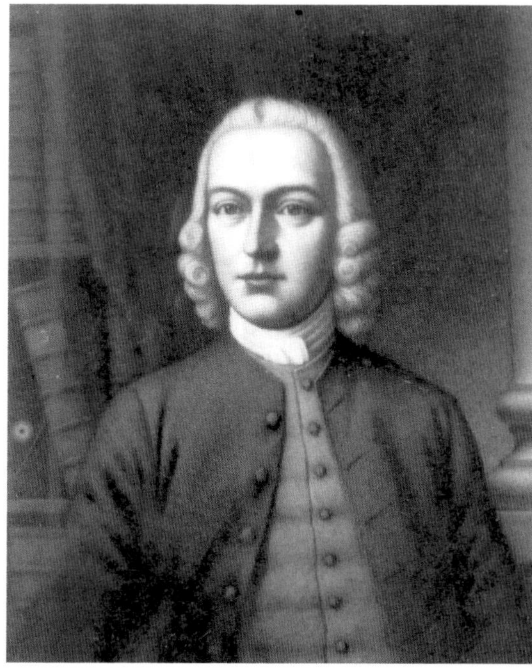

George Ross, who later would sign the Declaration of Independence, attended St. James Episcopal Church on the afternoon of the massacre. *Lancaster County Historical Society.*

Those with contacts in the Scots-Irish communities to the north filled in the background of the affair.

After returning to Paxton in mid-December, the Rangers had spent the better part of a fortnight stewing over the attack on Conestoga. Will Sock had escaped death and was under government custody with the remnant of the tribe in Lancaster. With Sock still at large, the Rangers must have considered the raid on Conestoga a failure. So they began talking of riding south again. Possibly on the night of December 20, some of them visited taverns in Donegal to enlist more help. Others must have carried the message to nearby Derry and Hanover townships and perhaps west of the Susquehanna. And slowly, one man here, another there, the Rangers gained commitments that expanded their force.

Early on the morning of December 27, between fifty and one hundred Rangers and fellow riders once again headed south. This time they probably followed the wider wagon road between Harris's Ferry and Lancaster. Dozens of wagons would have beaten down the snow, so the column could have traveled more easily, with two riders abreast.

The Rangers passed down Lancaster's snow-covered Queen Street at two o'clock that afternoon, just as the service at St. James was beginning. They skirted the twenty-five-year-old, cupola-topped county courthouse where laws had been passed and treaty councils had convened. They dismounted at the Sign of the White Swan. They tethered their horses in Coroner Slough's spacious stable yard. They gathered their weapons. Then the Rangers walked down King Street to the workhouse on what must have been a hard-pressed, slick snow pack. Scores of armed men striding through the borough in the middle of a workday afternoon would have created a fearsome scene for residents pursuing their workaday business.

When the Rangers reached the Prince Street intersection, they turned north and walked the short distance to the workhouse. There they encountered Sheriff Hay and Coroner Slough. Jailor Donnally was unaccountably absent. Slough, who had been at the Sign of the White Swan when the Rangers arrived, rather than joining in the service at St. James, had made a beeline for the workhouse. He barely beat the killers to their target; but then, along with Hay, without effective protest, he stepped aside.

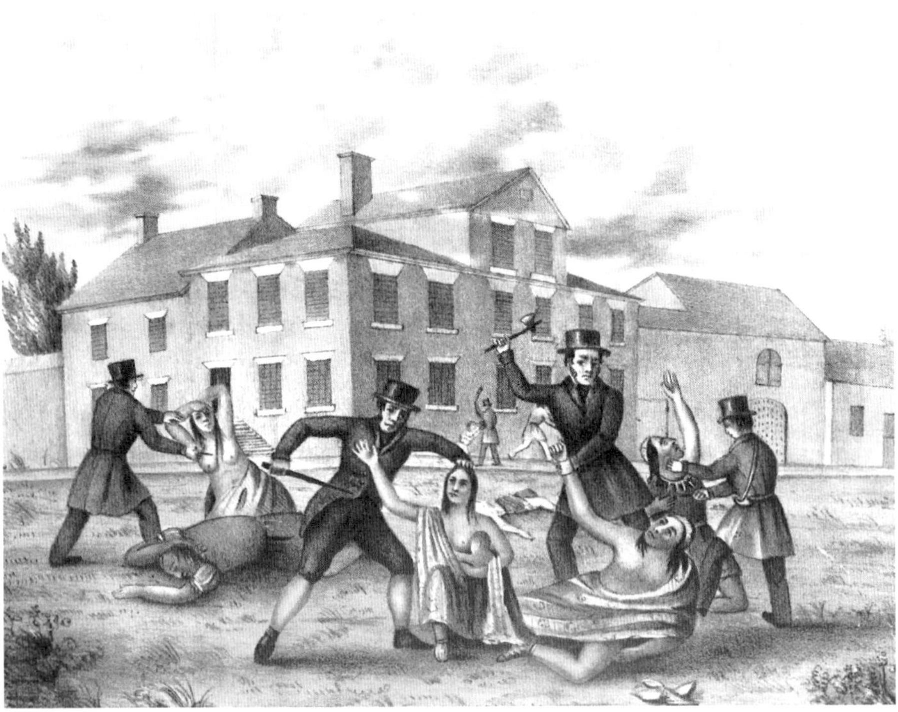

This largely inaccurate depiction of the massacre—a lithograph dated 1841—shows men in Victorian garb slaughtering half-naked Indians in freezing weather in front of Lancaster County Prison. *Library Company of Philadelphia.*

The Rangers broke open the workhouse door and pursued the fleeing Indians into the snow-filled yard. They hacked to death Will Sock and his wife and murdered two of the little girls over their dead bodies. They discharged a musket blast in another victim's mouth, splashing his brains on the yard wall. With tomahawks, they cut the hands and feet from several Indians. With knives, they scalped them all.

The bloodied killers emerged from the workhouse and walked back up King Street hill to the Swan. They mounted their horses and brazenly rode around the courthouse, shouting and discharging their firearms. Then they spurred their horses north on Queen Street toward home.

Justice Shippen reported that the entire affair lasted no more than twelve minutes.

CHAPTER 3

"The Same Spirit & Frantic Rage"

Many Lancaster residents did not condemn the Rangers' rampage, and some heartily endorsed the killing of accused enemy spies. After the hostilities of the French and Indian War and Pontiac's renewed atrocities, people living just inside the outer boundaries of the frontier understood the thirst for revenge among those living on the edge.

But other Lancastrians refused to excuse the brutal murder of defenseless women, children and old men. Moreover, thoughtful residents worried about the role some Lancaster officials may have played in the affair. How, they wondered, could dozens of men ride into the center of Lancaster in mid-afternoon and so easily massacre Indians supposedly under government protection?

On the evening of the attack, Magistrate Shippen and Sheriff Hay each wrote to Governor Penn to describe the grisly incident and to emphasize his lack of responsibility for what had happened.

Edward Shippen wrote of the Paxton Rangers: "All their business was done, and they were returning to their horses before I could get half way down to the Work House; the Sheriff and Coroner, however & several others, got down as soon as the Rioters, but could not prevail with them to stop their hands."

John Hay said the killers "left the Town without offering any insults to the Inhabitants, and without putting it in the power of any one to take or molest any of them without Danger of Life to the Person attempting it; of which both myself and the Coroner by our opposition were in great danger."

Meanwhile, Felix Donnally, the jail keeper, reappeared to take charge of burying the dead Indians. Undertakers laid the fourteen bodies on a wagon and dumped the load into a large hole dug at Nissly's, an old Mennonite family cemetery on Cherry Alley, a block north of the Episcopal church. When Donnally gave Hay an itemized bill for fourteen pounds and nine shillings for food, firewood and other services provided to the Indians at the workhouse, he left blank an amount for "the Trouble and Expense of having the said Fourteen Indians carried to the grave and interred."

Accounts of the second massacre reached the general public in Philadelphia faster than news of the first, although events were not always reported correctly. In his December 29 journal entry, Henry Melchior Muhlenberg, patriarch of the Lutheran Church in America, claimed that the Paxton Boys had killed the Indians in the workhouse because those Indians had murdered the Indians at Conestoga. Along with some others outside the pacifist sects, Muhlenberg seemed eager to claim that the Conestogas, one way or another, were responsible for their own deaths.

But Philadelphia's Quaker community was appalled. Samuel Foulke, a Quaker member of the assembly, recorded in his journal on January 2, 1764, that an "Audacious Club of Villains, all well mounted, Enter'd the town, broke Open the prison Door, & in Cool blood inhumanly butcher'd all ye Indians, being 14 men, women & Children!"

A fear that agitated frontiersmen might extend their attack to other peaceful Indians, however, quickly upstaged concerns about the Conestogas. Before leaving Lancaster, the Paxton Rangers had informed bystanders that they had not yet finished with Pennsylvania's protected Indians. They claimed they would move on to Philadelphia and there attack the 125 Moravian Indians who had settled on an island in the Delaware.

When Philadelphians learned of this threat, they worried about what the Paxtonians might do to the Indians. But they also were concerned about what they might do to the Indians' Quaker friends and the entire government structure the Rangers held responsible for not doing enough to protect frontier families.

John Penn met with the Pennsylvania Provincial Council on December 29, after which he wrote letters to John Elder, John Armstrong and Shippen. He asked Elder to provide information about the killers and to "continue to use your best Endeavours to discourage & Suppress all Insurrections" in Lancaster County.

Penn did not blame Elder outright for the massacres at Conestoga and Lancaster. Nevertheless, without explanation, he relieved the minister of

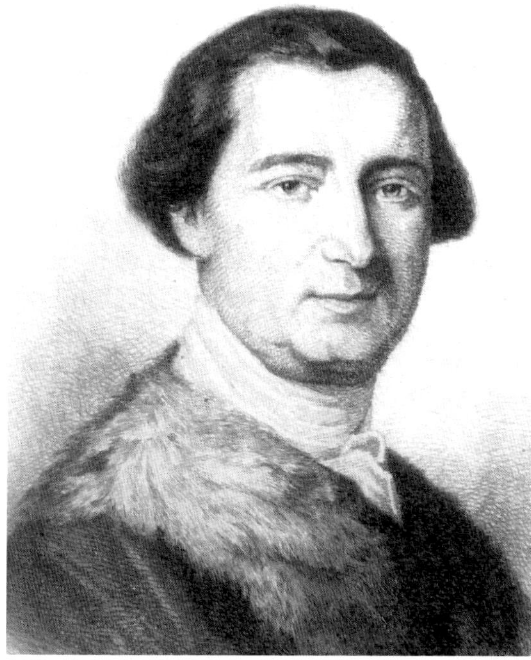

John Penn served as governor of Pennsylvania during the Paxton Boys' uprising. *Historical Society of Pennsylvania.*

command of the Paxton Rangers and ordered him to turn over his arms and ammunition to Captain Asher Clayton, his replacement.

In his letter to Armstrong, Penn insisted that most of the "Rioters" lived on the "frontiers of Cumberland & Lancaster Counties." He said that if Armstrong were diligent in his inquiry, "you will soon make a Discovery of them, as they could not assemble & march in Bodies thro' the Country without being seen & known by a great Number of people."

Penn also asked Shippen to discover the names of the Rangers' ringleaders and their further designs. The government, he assured the Lancaster magistrate, would protect the Indians on Province Island while attempting to apprehend "the people who have committed these shocking Cruelties at Lancaster." Replying immediately, Shippen said he and the other magistrates would do all they could to discover who had killed the Indians. He added, "I dread the Consequences of the Rioters going down to the Province Island."

Writing to Penn at greater length and more defensively on January 5, Shippen argued against charges that Lancaster's officials could have prevented the slaughter. He denied that any of the magistrates had advance knowledge of the Paxton Rangers' plans and claimed that he did not know

Captain Robertson's troops were in the borough. In any case, he added, those soldiers could not have been summoned in time to save the Indians.

Penn delivered a second punitive proclamation on January 2. He denounced the men who "violently broke open the Work House" and butchered Indians "who had been taken under the immediate Care and Protection of the Magistrates of the said County." He charged all civil and military officials to find the killers, who had acted "in violation of the Public Faith, & in Defiance of all Law." And this time he offered a substantial reward of two hundred pounds for information leading to conviction of each "ringleader." Further, he said, any accomplice who identified a leader would receive a reward and a pardon.

In letters to Benjamin Franklin, Sir William Johnson and other officials three days later, Penn described the Conestogas' killers as "wicked People" and "riotous Parties" who threatened to extend the "barbarous outrage" and "horrid Violence's" they had perpetrated on the Conestogas to the Moravian Indians.

Shippen, while also professing concern that the murderers remained at large, seemed much more worried about what they might do than what they had done. He said so in extensive letters to his son-in-law, Colonel James Burd, who was then commanding troops at Fort Augusta, ninety miles north of Lancaster. If the Paxton Rangers tried to assault the Philadelphia Indians—and the city's residents opposed the frontiersmen—Shippen wrote, "God only knows where this Tragical affair will terminate. I fear the Consequences; yet I am hoping it will not bring on a Civil war." Shippen also told Burd he was concerned about the Iroquois, who would be "exasperated to the last degree" by the murder of the Conestogas, "and pretending to make Peace is all they will do in order to get us into a Noose."

Meanwhile, Penn attempted to move the Moravian Indians to New York for their protection. Fearing they might meet the fate of the Conestogas, the Indians were eager to go. Penn ordered Robertson's Highlanders, recently removed from Lancaster, to march the Indians through New Jersey. But New York's governor, Cadwalader Colden, halted the procession at his colony's border, rejecting the refugees because "the Indians on the East side of the Susquehanna are the most obnoxious to the People of this Province of any, having done the most mischief." So the Lenapes trudged back to Philadelphia, where they were lodged in the city's military barracks at Second and Green Streets, guarded by a regiment of British regulars and insulted by Philadelphians who blamed them for causing the crisis.

The Paxton Rangers took their time, cultivating concern about the Moravian Indians in order to convert greater numbers to their cause.

The expanded edition of Rangers included not only Scots-Irish but also many Germans and several English. They called themselves "Hickory Boys," perhaps after Lancaster's early name, Hickory Town, or because they wanted to be viewed as hardened frontiersmen. But the Rangers from Paxton remained the nucleus of the force, and "Paxton Boys" became their popular designation.[4]

Late in January, the Philadelphia merchant Benjamin Kendall encountered Robert Fulton Sr. in a tavern outside Lancaster. Kendall, an English Quaker, reported that the Scots-Irish Presbyterian Fulton had claimed 1,500 men were preparing to march on Philadelphia. If that force was insufficient, Fulton had said, 5,000 could be assembled to attack the Indians and their protectors. Fulton also had said the Paxtonians would not turn back because "they were of the same Spirit with the blood-ran, blood-thirsty Presbyterians, who cut off King Charles his Head."

"I hear you intend to kill the Quakers," Kendall had said.

"No," Kendall said Fulton had replied, "but they or any others who should oppose them they would kill."

Such accounts of the Paxton Boys' imminent intentions severely alarmed the government. On January 28, the provincial council advised the governor to order troops guarding the Moravian Indians "to fire upon any body of armed Men who should make their appearance in an hostile manner." The next day, Penn ordered a royal regiment at Carlisle to move to Lancaster and hold itself ready to march wherever it might be needed.

Any idea of intimidating the insurrection near its home base failed. By the first of February, the Paxton Boys were primed. John Elder told Colonel Joseph Shippen that an armed force was preparing to march on Philadelphia, and it would be "useless if not dangerous to act in opposition to an enraged multitude."

And so the Conestogas' killers and several hundred others, dressed in homespun clothing and carrying deadly weapons, marched east to do more damage. Many Philadelphians viewed the coming horde as the vanguard of a potentially fearsome frontier rebellion.

The largest city in the colonies—ten times larger than Lancaster—was a tempting target. Philadelphia's twenty thousand residents included most of the colony's movers and shakers. The Paxton Boys might have hoped to create a wave in Philadelphia that would wash across Pennsylvania.

Long dominated by antiwar Quakers and thought by most residents to be well insulated from frontier violence, Philadelphia had no standing militia. Penn was wary of employing royal troops to counter the Paxton Boys, lest he spark a civil war. So he and those members of the Pennsylvania Assembly who did not flee the beleaguered city summoned a volunteer army.

With Benjamin Franklin's aid, Penn took charge of more than five hundred hastily armed citizens. Most were English, including some Quakers who approved of defending the home turf. But members of Philadelphia Monthly Meeting who took up muskets disgusted Philadelphians who believed pacifist politics were largely responsible for provoking the Paxtonians. Here were those Quakers, they said, again protecting Indians when they would do nothing to protect frontier settlers.

Penn divided the makeshift militia into infantry, cavalry and artillery units. The temporary soldiers constructed fortifications on Market Square, between the Paxton Boys' line of march and the Indians in the barracks. They positioned their cannon and waited.

The Paxton Boys moved closer.

On February 3, the assembly passed a riot act targeting the marchers. The act ordered the death penalty for any group of twelve or more "turbulent and evil-minded persons" who refused to disperse.

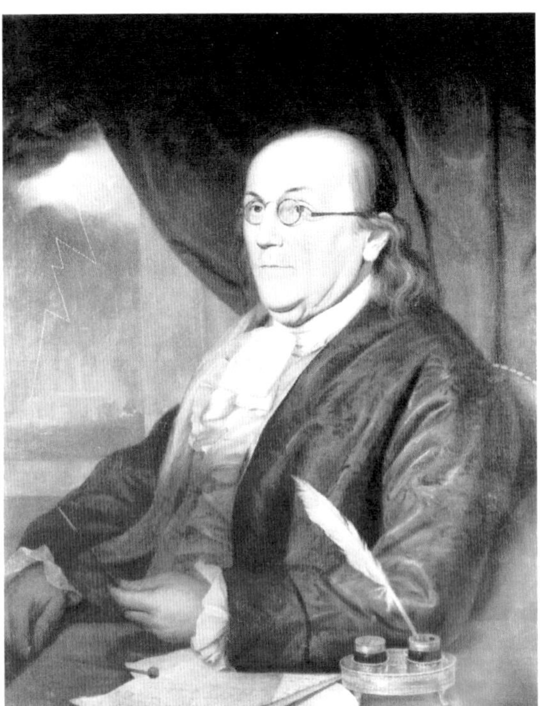

Benjamin Franklin helped defuse a crisis when the Paxton Boys marched on Philadelphia. Portrait by Charles Wilson Peale. *Historical Society of Pennsylvania.*

On February 4, the governor addressed the assembly:

> *I am sorry to inform you that the same Spirit & frantic Rage, which actuated those who lately put to death the Indians in Lancaster County, Still prevails among them, & that, instead of having any Remorse for, or in the least dreading the bad Consequences of their Conduct, I have just reason to believe they are daily strengthening their Party.*

On the evening of February 5, the Paxton Boys crossed the Schuylkill River and camped for the night at Germantown, just northwest of Philadelphia. Rumors filtering into the city suggested that the frontiersmen had scheduled their attack for the next morning.

David Rittenhouse, the celebrated scientist and brother-in-law of Lancaster's Anglican minister, Thomas Barton, wrote the most vivid account of the Paxton Boys as viewed from his workshop window in Germantown. "I have seen hundreds of Indians travelling the country," he wrote, "and can with truth affirm, that the behaviour of these fellows was ten times more savage and brutal than theirs." According to Rittenhouse, the vigilantes ran the muzzles of their guns through windows to frighten women and brazenly attacked men, "dragging them by their hair to the ground, and pretending to scalp them."

Just before dawn on February 6, the defenders of Philadelphia formed a battle line on Market Square. Someone fired a cannon. A volunteer began a steady drum roll. Church bells rang an alarm. Householders put candles in their windows so the troops would have light to see the enemy.

But then, except for shopkeepers losing a day of business and householders a bit of tallow, nothing happened. Informed of the armed resistance facing them and counseled by clergymen to back off, the Paxton Boys decided to camp in place and negotiate.

On the morning of February 7, Franklin, along with Philadelphia's mayor, Pennsylvania's attorney general and other officials, rode to Germantown to present the government's position. There they met Matthew Smith and James Gibson, the leading representatives and chief negotiators of the Paxton Boys. Colonel Armstrong accompanied them. As chief negotiator for the government, Franklin told the Paxton Boys that they would meet massive resistance if they attacked Philadelphia. This "fighting face," as Franklin termed it, encouraged the Paxtonians to negotiate.

After meeting for several hours, the two sides came to terms. Most of the Paxton Boys would return home without creating further distress. Smith and Gibson would remain to present the group's formal grievances. Franklin's

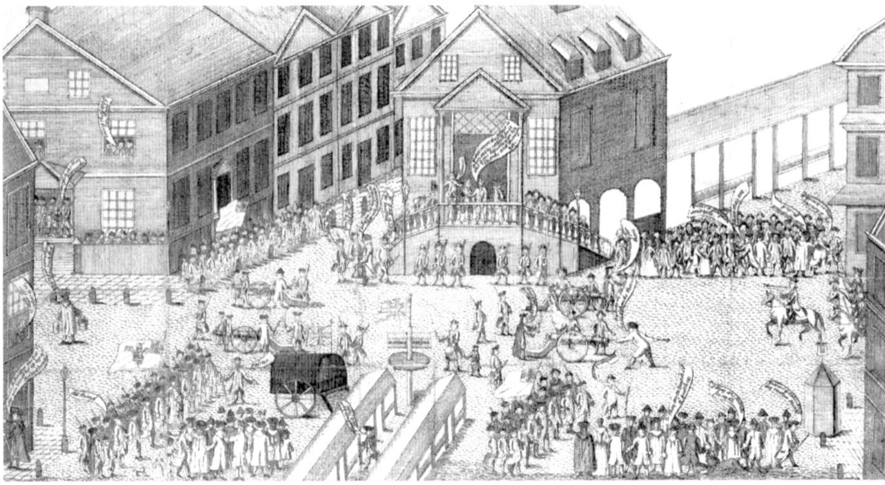

One of the first American political cartoons, drawn by Henry Dawkins in 1764, depicts Philadelphia's preparations to repel the Paxton Boys. The State House stands in background. *Library Company of Pennsylvania.*

delegation pledged that the governor and assembly would consider these complaints with dispatch.

A week later, Smith and Gibson presented their written defense of the vigilantes' actions. The Paxton Boys had composed "A Declaration" before arriving in Germantown. Smith and Gibson completed a "Remonstrance" on February 13. Both documents were later published as *A Declaration and Remonstrance of the Distressed and Bleeding Frontier Inhabitants of the Province of Pennsylvania.*

The documents identified the Paxton Boys as inhabitants not only of Lancaster County but also of York and Cumberland Counties to the west and Berks and Northampton Counties to the north.

The "Declaration" claimed that "invidious Representations" of the killings at Conestoga and Lancaster had encouraged greater censure than the facts warranted. The Conestogas were in league with "our openly avowed embittered Enemy." The government supported and protected these Indians "while at the same Time hundreds of poor distressed Families of his Majesty's Subjects...were left to starve neglected." The document concluded that no one should think it strange that taxing residents to pay for supporting the Moravian Indians "should awaken the Resentment of a People grossly abused, unrighteously burdened, and made Dupes and Slaves to Indians."

The "Remonstrance" listed nine grievances. Foremost was that citizens of Philadelphia, Chester and Bucks Counties had greater representation in the Quaker-dominated assembly than citizens of Lancaster and other frontier counties; therefore, the government was not responsive to frontier concerns. Secondarily, the document denounced an assembly proposal to move a trial for the Conestogas' killers from Lancaster to Philadelphia.[5]

Other grievances expressed long-held desires to expel the Moravian Indians from Pennsylvania; provide government assistance for men wounded in the Indian wars; reinstate a government reward for collecting Indian scalps that had been in effect during part of the French and Indian War; suspend trade with Indians until they released white captives; forbid Quakers from holding their own treaty sessions with Indians; and encourage the garrison at Fort Augusta to do more to protect the frontier.

In the "Remonstrance," the Paxton Boys argued that all Indians represented the enemy. "In what Nation under the Sun," they wrote, "was it ever the Custom, that when a neighboring Nation took up Arms, not an individual of the Nation should be touched, but only the Persons that offered Hostilities? Who ever proclaimed War with a part of a Nation, and not with the Whole?"

Smith and Gibson might have saved their ink and a week of work because the government ignored most of their very public demands. Quaker scribes replied with a lengthy defense of their Indian policy, but Penn and the assembly spent the rest of February disagreeing over who should take the lead in responding to the Paxton Boys. The assembly proposed to examine the complaints before a joint session of the assembly and provincial council, with the governor in attendance. But Penn turned down the idea as "unbecoming the Honour and Dignity of the Government."

Pennsylvania eventually ignored all of the Paxton Boys' concerns but one. In July, the government established premiums for capturing or scalping hostile Indians. More than half a year after the Paxton Rangers took Conestoga scalps, knowing they would receive no monetary reward, the commonwealth agreed to spur frontier initiative by giving vigilantes twice the scalp bounty offered to soldiers. Scalps of males older than ten would earn 134 Spanish dollars, scalps of females older than ten would earn 50. Live prisoners were worth even more.[6]

But the Paxton Boys won something more immediate and far more valuable before they left eastern Pennsylvania that February. After delivering their documents, Smith and Gibson met alone with Penn. A month later,

Franklin charged that Penn had stopped trying to find the Conestogas' killers and instead was "answering the Deputies of the Rioters privately."

No one recorded the conversation of Penn, Smith and Gibson. Future events suggest, however, that all parties left that meeting with an understanding that no one in the provincial government was going to work overtime trying to pinpoint blame for the massacre in Lancaster County.

CHAPTER 4

"Persons of Undoubted Probity & Veracity"

As the winter of 1764 progressed, it became increasingly clear that all of John Penn's rhetoric aimed at arresting and punishing the Conestogas' killers was as empty as William Penn's "one Head & one Heart" pledge ultimately proved to be.

The Paxton Boys returned to their farms and went about their business without disturbance from any authority. By spring, the men who had brutally slaughtered twenty Indians in their huts at Conestoga and in the workhouse yard at Lancaster realized they had escaped punishment.

The British statesman Lord Halifax viewed the massacre as a serious breach of colonial justice. He condemned "the horrid murders committed by some People of Pennsylvania" and ordered General Thomas Gage, then in charge of British armies in North America, to assist the Pennsylvania government in "bringing to condign Punishment the Perpetrators." In response, however, Pennsylvania's government merely went through the motions of seeking justice.

John Penn delivered two proclamations condemning "barbarous" behavior in defiance of government. He issued arrest warrants and offered a major reward for information leading to conviction. He lectured magistrates and ministers in Lancaster and nearby counties on the importance of stopping the insurgents before they further undermined the rule of law. All of these proclamations and warrants, rewards and lectures resulted in nothing more than a new disrespect for the rule of law on the frontier.

Operating in a separate hemisphere of futility, Quakers in the assembly demanded that Penn do more to identify the Paxton Boys by ordering the sheriff, coroner and magistrates of Lancaster "to come down and give you the best information that can be obtained of the Persons concerned in these violences." But this proposal died after the provincial council argued that bringing Lancaster County officials to Philadelphia "would be attended with many ill Consequences." Instead, the council advised, Penn should ask trustworthy justices "to examine upon Oath the Sheriff and Coroner & any others, respecting their knowledge of the Authors and Perpetrators of the late Murders committed on the Indians there, and do this with all possible Secrecy."

So on February 4, the day before the Paxton Boys arrived in Germantown, Penn wrote to "request" Lancaster magistrates Edward Shippen, Emanuel Carpenter and Isaac Sanders to call before them the sheriff, coroner and any others who might have information about the murderers, especially their names. He told them to collect written depositions and to assure any informants that their identities would be protected.

Chief magistrate Shippen controlled the county's judiciary. Carpenter and Sanders, in addition to being magistrates, were two of the county's four representatives to the assembly. These men, if any, should have been expected to "make a full Discovery," as Penn phrased it, of who murdered the Conestogas.

But Shippen, Carpenter and Sanders ignored Penn's directive. They followed an established pattern of passivity among Lancaster County officials toward anything related to the killing of the Conestogas. The coroner's inquest after the massacre at Indian Town had identified none of the perpetrators, and there is no record that Shippen ordered any investigation following the massacre at the workhouse.

More than six weeks after the killings, the Lancaster magistrates must have known the identity of at least some of the murderers without formally deposing anyone. After they left Indian Town in flames, the Rangers had talked at some length with Thomas Wright and Robert Barber. Scores, if not hundreds, of borough residents had observed the raiders as they marched to and from the slaughter at the workhouse. Moreover, Shippen had reported in a letter on December 19, 1763, that a number of "the Indian Murderers" approached Assemblyman James Wright at the Susquehanna ferry and told him they planned to march on Philadelphia to kill the Moravian Indians. This was more than a week before the workhouse massacre. The killers were not hiding.

The names of the leaders of these men must have been known to the Reverend John Elder, commander of and minister to many of them, and to John Harris Jr., who had helped organize some of them during the French and Indian War. With aid from Elder and Harris, if not employing their own resources, the magistrates easily could have made a list of prime suspects.

But the magistrates never identified anyone. The Indian killers all remained "persons unknown." The magistrates never even deposed Coroner Slough and Sheriff Hay, as Penn had requested. Nor did they officially question anyone else who may have been able to identify the killers. There is no record of Lancaster County's judiciary ever doing anything to "make a full Discovery."

Instead, according to early sources, the magistrates collected affidavits from residents who had reason to despise Indians. These affidavits are not included in court records, but apparent copies appeared in two places in the winter of 1764 as part of a manuscript titled *The Apology of the Paxton Volunteers Addressed to the Candid & Impartial World* and as footnotes to a pro–Paxton Boys printed pamphlet titled *The Conduct of the Paxton-Men.* The texts of the two sets of affidavits are similar, but not exact, although both were presented in a fashion that suggests they were copied verbatim from a record.[7]

The *Apology* listed six affidavits and the *Conduct* eight. Altogether, nine different persons provided testimony. None of these affidavits is dated, and no original copies are known to exist. The author of the *Apology* said that the testimony was collected "at different Times, before different Magistrates & by Persons of undoubted Probity & Veracity" and that "any Person that will take the Trouble may collect as many more of the same Kind as he pleases."

None of the affidavits mentioned the Rangers. Most cast blame on the Conestogas, often individual Indians. Some castigated Indians in general. All deponents lived in Lancaster County, including at least two in Paxton. Five were Scots-Irish. All had experienced negative encounters with Indians, including two who had been held captive by Indians and one whose brother-in-law had been killed by an Indian.

Three magistrates—Thomas Forster, of Paxton, and Robert Thompson and James Bickham, both of Lancaster—gathered these documents. Thompson, a retired physician of Scots-Irish heritage, and Bickham, the chief burgess and a liquor dealer in the borough, took all their testimony in Lancaster. Forster, a Scots-Irish neighbor of Harris and a parishioner and close friend of John Elder, deposed the residents of Paxton.

The most prominent of the Indian haters was the German Colonel John Hambright, operator of a Lancaster brewery. Early in the French and Indian

War, he had led a contingent of local farmers to Philadelphia demanding assistance to defend the countryside. Later he served as an officer at Fort Augusta, once being ordered explicitly to "kill, scalp, and captivate as many (Indians) as you can." He had accompanied Matthias Slough to the coroner's inquisition at Indian Town.

Hambright provided purely circumstantial evidence concerning Will Sock. He told Justice Thompson that on a mission away from Fort Augusta in 1757, he had hailed Sock, but the Indian and a companion had run away. Later Hambright discovered that an "Old Man" had been killed in that area the day before. So Sock and his companion "were suspected & believed to be the Perpetrators of that Murder."

Bickham took a statement from another German, Abraham Newcomer, who was the only Mennonite to testify. The Hempfield Township gunsmith had a personal reason to dislike Indians. His family blamed Indians for killing Newcomer's brother-in-law, Joseph Gochnauer, just before the massacre at Conestoga. But Newcomer did not mention that in his testimony.

The gunsmith claimed Sock and another Conestoga, Indian John, had threatened to scalp him "as soon as they would a Dog." He also said that several days before the Conestoga raid, Sock had asked Newcomer to repair a tomahawk and when he had refused Sock said, "I'll have it mended to your Sorrow."

Bickham also heard testimony from a woman who had suffered an ugly personal encounter with Indians. In the Penn's Creek Massacre of 1755, Indians killed and burned the body of Jean Jacques LeRoy, a Swiss settler. They captured his daughter, Marie or Anne Marie, then about twelve, along with her brother and children from other families. Marie LeRoy escaped in 1759 and, after describing her trials in a pamphlet, became a frontier celebrity. In 1764, she was about twenty-one years old and a recent arrival in Lancaster.

LeRoy eagerly told Bickham stories about her captivity. She had seen Conestogas come and go in her Indian village and had been told they were hostile to the English. LeRoy said Will Sock's mother had claimed Sock "was good for Nothing, or Words to the Purpose." And an Indian named Jo Compass, whom LeRoy later observed at the 1762 Indian treaty held at Lancaster, had admitted killing several people.

Three other Lancastrians talked briefly with Bickham. Thomas Moore said that during his six years of captivity "strange Messenger Indians…that lived Among the White People" brought news of the movements of English troops. Patrick Agnew, who had served as a constable during the 1762 treaty session, said the governor had ordered him to proclaim that no one in the town should sell liquor to Indians. According to Agnew, Teedyuscung, the Lenape leader who was killed in April 1763, damned the governor and "offere'd Violence to this Deponent." One "Mrs. Thompson" told Bickham that Will Sock had threatened her, saying, "I kill you, and all Lancaster cannot catch me" and "this Place (meaning Lancaster) is mine and I will have it yet."

Thomas Forster heard similar testimony from three men.

Alexander Stephens, a Scots-Irish Presbyterian from Paxton (and, incidentally, grandfather and namesake of the future vice president of the Confederate States of America), traded with the Indians. According to a family source, Stephens lived among Indians and may have married an Indian. Stephens later married a white woman and served at Fort Augusta during the French and Indian War. In his deposition, he said he had heard that the Conestogas had killed an Indian named Jegrea "because he would not go to war," and that another Indian, James Cottes, had admitted that he had helped kill several white people.[8]

Robert Armstrong, a Scots-Irishman whose house north of Paxton had been destroyed by Indians, testified that Sheehays and a nephew, Isaac, had been "so impudent as to say (in 1762), that they had been at War with the White People & would soon be at War again." Armstrong also said that other Indians stayed at his place for several days "& proved very insolent," stealing corn and fruit and killing hogs.

Forster's final affidavit provider, the Scots-Irish Presbyterian Charles Cunningham, said only that he had heard "an Indian named Joshua James say since the last War, that he never killed a White Man in his Life, but six Duch Men" in New Jersey.

Aside from hearsay about Indians serving as hostile messengers, killing unnamed white people and making wild threats, nothing in these affidavits clearly indicts the Conestogas for crimes against settlers. It is difficult to imagine any of these statements standing up in court.[9]

A further accusation printed in the *Apology* relies on similar hearsay. The authors of that tract said "a Person of unquestionable Veracity" heard George Sock tell a "strange Indian" during the Lancaster treaty session that he had killed six white men during the war, "upon which the other Indian rose up, took him by the Hand & drank to him as to a Brother."[10]

Nothing in these accusations relates in any way to Penn's request that the magistrates obtain information about the men who had killed the Conestogas.

When Lancaster's magistrates failed to identify, let alone charge or try, the Indians' assailants, critics assailed the Pennsylvania Supreme Court for not exerting more influence over local judges. In response, the high court said it would consider appointing an assistant judge to help deal with frontier issues in the future. John Penn wrote to his brother, Thomas, in March 1764 to say that Philadelphians approved of an additional justice "being apprehensive lest a further delay [of justice in Lancaster County] might create some uneasiness among the people." But Penn was referring to uneasiness among white frontiersmen, whose cases were backing up as the supreme court concentrated on Philadelphia and its neighboring counties. By March, justice for the Conestogas was no longer a pressing issue.

The ongoing war with Indians aroused by Pontiac's Rebellion also trumped justice in Lancaster. Following Pontiac's initial spectacular success in capturing forts and overrunning settlements along the Great Lakes, through Ohio and well into Pennsylvania, the British Ministry aggressively fought back. As a result, raids on Paxton and nearby settlements all but ended in 1764. Some frontier residents pointed to the restoration of peace as vindication for ending the Conestogas' ability to provide inside information to hostiles. Safety for frontier families, they believed, justified the massacre.

In addition, many officials in Philadelphia and Lancaster had a political reason to avoid punishing the killers. At the expense of Quakers and pacifist Germans, the more militant Germans and Scots-Irish had assumed greater power in the early 1760s. Those who wanted to gain or retain power found it useful, especially on the frontier, to sympathize with the Paxton Boys' grievances and excuse or even defend the Conestogas' slaughter. These interests were rewarded with victory in the 1764 elections.

But the government did not completely ignore Indian concerns. Even as they failed to deliver justice for the Conestogas, Penn and other officials worried about how the killings might influence other Indians, especially the powerful Iroquois. Sir William Johnson, superintendent of Indian Affairs in the Northern Department, told Penn he was concerned that the incident would "stagger the affections" of the Iroquois. After meeting with Iroquois representatives in February 1764, Johnson told Penn he had "assured them of your resolutions to bring the Offenders to punishment."

Indians living within Pennsylvania's white settlements never trusted the government to sanction the Conestogas' killers or to protect other Indians. Many Lenapes fled the state. Immediately after the massacre, Hannah Freeman and other Indians residing in Chester County moved to a Quaker community in New Jersey. Writing from Fort Hunter, north of Harrisburg, in February 1764, Samuel Hunter told Edward Shippen that an Indian man named William Peters feared for his safety after the Paxton Boys marched on Philadelphia. Hunter assigned a guard to protect Peters.

Repercussions from the massacre continued for many years. At treaty sessions, the Iroquois cited the fate of the Conestogas as reason enough not to trust white negotiators. John Heckewelder, the Moravian missionary, reported that the Lenapes believed Indian-settler relations had been poisoned because the Conestogas' "blood ran in streams into our (treaty council) fire, and extinguished it so entirely, that not one spark was left us whereby to kindle a new fire."

Early in the Revolutionary War, Lenapes converted by Moravians and displaced in Ohio declined proffered aid from the Continental Congress because they feared the government might "protect" them as it had the Conestogas. And these Ohio Lenapes, many of them Moravian Indians who had escaped the Paxton Boys' march on Philadelphia, eventually served as another object lesson for all Indians.

Ever since their confinement in the Philadelphia barracks, the Moravian Indians had suffered from a white backlash. In early March of 1764, General Gage told Penn not to release the Indians from the barracks. He said he feared they might tell the Iroquois stories "Prejudicial to our Affairs. The resentment of those Savages must be Strong against us for the miserable Fate of the poor Wretches who were murdered at Lancaster, and for the attempt made on their own lives." Angry frontiersmen issued more direct warnings, burning the Indians' villages near Bethlehem and threatening their lives if they tried to return to the area. So the Indians remained in the barracks, where they suffered a smallpox outbreak in the summer of 1764 that killed nearly sixty.

In the spring of 1765, Moravian missionaries led the remaining eighty-three Indians to Iroquois land on the Susquehanna's North Branch. When the Iroquois sold the land out from under them, these Indians moved even farther west, to the Muskingum Valley of eastern Ohio. There they settled with other Lenapes converted by Moravians at a place called Gnadenhutten, or "Huts of Grace."

During the Revolutionary War, the Moravian Indians repeatedly warned frontier settlements of British movements. Nevertheless, many settlers believed the Lenapes were allied with hostile Indians who supported the British and attacked outlying farms.

In the late winter of 1782, a raiding party of Indians from the Detroit area murdered a white family in western Pennsylvania. On their way home, the raiders stopped briefly at Gnadenhutten. In retaliation for this perceived hospitality extended to murderers, a large group of Pennsylvanians under the command of Lieutenant Colonel David Williamson decided to attack the Lenapes.

The innocent and unsuspecting Indians, many of them children, warmly welcomed Williamson and his men when they arrived in early March, but Williamson ordered the Indians disarmed, separated by gender and locked in two meetinghouses. On the morning of March 8, the militiamen methodically crushed the Indians' skulls, one by one, with wooden mallets. Then they scalped them.

The next day Williamson's men went to the nearby settlement of Salem, captured more Indians, disarmed them, stripped them naked, brought them to Gnadenhutten, crushed their skulls and scalped them. Then Williamson's soldiers looted the Indians' dwellings, which they renamed—appropriately, if prosaically—"slaughter houses."

Troubled by the freelance actions of a frontier militia, Congress ordered Pennsylvania and Virginia to investigate the killing of nearly one hundred Indians at Gnadenhutten. These investigations ended almost as quickly and inconclusively as the counterfeit search for the Conestogas' killers, and Congress moved on to other matters.

PART 2

Retelling the Story

CHAPTER 5

"I Never Heard One Word of It Till It Was Just Over"

Comprehensive description and analysis of the anti-Indian violence in December 1763 in Lancaster County is problematic. A conspiracy of silence among the Paxton Rangers, coupled with the Conestogas' annihilation, take all of the primary actors out of the picture. There were no newspapers in Lancaster to report the two massacres. The two Philadelphia papers published John Penn's proclamations denouncing the Indian killers but not a line of type about the massacres themselves.

The most complete contemporary account is contained in letters Edward Shippen wrote to John Penn and others. But while Shippen's letters seem to provide a detailed description of events, they are transparently self-serving. Under fire for not preventing the killings or arresting the killers, Lancaster's chief magistrate wrote overtime, attempting to deflect blame. He posted his letters at Matthias Slough's White Swan and wagons carried the letters to Philadelphia and elsewhere.

In a letter to Penn on the evening of December 14, Shippen explained what he knew about the massacre at Conestoga earlier that day.

> *One Robert Edgar, a hired Man to Captain Thomas McKee, living near the Borough, acquainted me to-day that a Company of People from the Frontiers had killed and scalped most of the Indians at the Conestogoe Town early this Morning; he said he had his information from an Indian boy who made his Escape; Mr. Slough has been to the place and held a Coroner's Inquest on the Corpses, being Six in number; Bill Sawk and*

> *some other Indians were gone towards Smith's Iron Works to sell brooms; but where they are now we can't understand; And the Indians, John Smith, & Peggy, his Wife, and their child, and Young Joe Hays, were abroad last night too, and lodged at one Peter Swar's, about two miles from hence; These last came here this afternoon, whom we acquainted with what had happened to their Friends & Relations, and advised them to put themselves under our Protection, which they readily agreed to; And they are now in our Work House by themselves, where they are well provided for with every necessary. Warrants are issued for the apprehending of the Murderers, said to be upwards of fifty men, well armed & mounted.*[11]

On December 16, Shippen wrote to John Elder and James Burd. He told Elder, then still commanding and ministering to the Paxton Rangers, that the attack would be "very strictly inquired into and resented according to the seriousness of the offence." He told Burd, his son-in-law, that the Conestogas' killers "are resolved to justify the action." He did not reveal how he knew the thoughts of these unidentified murderers two days after the massacre.

Shippen also was first to describe the December 27 slaughter. That evening, he wrote to John Penn, informing him that "upwards of a hundred armed men, from the Westward, rode very fast into Town, turned their Horses into Mr. Slough's Yard, and proceeded with the greatest Precipitation to the Work House, stove open the door and killed all the Indians, and then took to their horses and rode off."

On January 5, Shippen wrote the most complete account of the workhouse massacre in a letter to his son, Joseph. The magistrate reported what he had done following the first massacre. Then he explained what had happened in Lancaster, beginning with events on Tuesday, December 20, one week before the attack, and ending with his "best excuse I can make for the Magistrates."

> *On Tuesday night between 8 and 9 o Clock, Donnally the Prison Keeper came to my house, and said he was informed, a parcel of the Rioters who had killed the Conestogoe Indians at the Mannor, were collected together at a Tavern on the Donegal Road about four or five miles off, who were to be joined by a larger Number before Midnight, & then they were to come in a Body, & break open the Workhouse, and kill all the Indians… And after Some Consultation, we came to a Resolution to call the two Constables of the Borough, and to send them out as Spies to a Couple of Taverns about the distances above mentioned, and to bring us word as Soon*

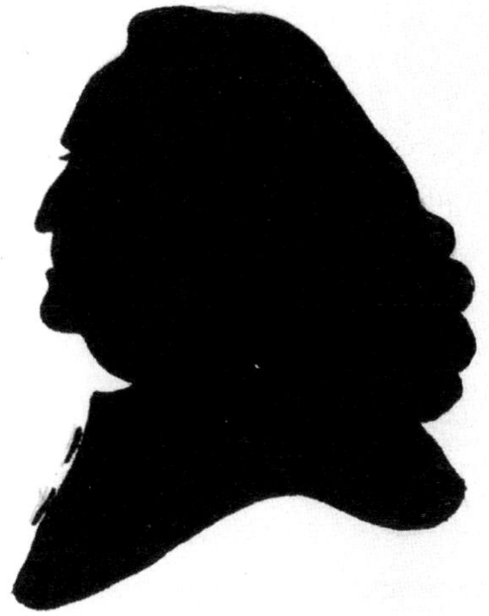

Silhouette of Edward Shippen, an early mayor of Philadelphia and later chief magistrate of Lancaster County. *Historical Society of Pennsylvania.*

as possible; and if on their Return, we found the Story true, we Should immediately alarmn the Borough; and do the best we could to prevent the Indians being killed; tho' God knows, the Inhabitants, undisciplined, & miserably armed, could have made but a poor Stand against 80 or 100 Desperadoes well armed at least, and in the dark, too, the Streets being full of Snow & ice, and the weather excessive cold; and at that time I had not heard of any Commanding Officer with his Highlanders Soldiers being in the Borough. However the Justices Stay'd together till one o'Clock in the morning, when the Constables returned, almost perished with the Cold, and gave us the pleasure to hear that there were no Rioters at either of those Places, nor had any of them been seen thereabouts Since they came from the Conestogoe Town. After this, we were in hopes we Should have no more disturbance from those People till they, Some days afterwards, rushed into the Town at Noonday on horseback with their Muskets, Tomahawks, & Scalping knives, broke open the work house and killed the Indians, before we knew whereabouts we were; for it was said, they were not more than eleven or twelve Minutes perpetrating that Tragical scene. And I declare for my part, I never heard one word of it till it was just over, and the Rioters were returning from the bloody Place where the Indians were; So that if the Magistrates & Burgesses had thought of calling upon Captain Robinson [sic] *for assistance, it could have been of no service; as his Men were mostly billotted up and down the town (as we understood) and quite off their guard. This is a faithful Account of the affair, and is the best excuse I can make for the Magistrates and therefore conclude.*

Two other Lancaster County men also wrote self-protecting letters about the massacres. On December 16, Elder told Penn he had tried to stop the attack on Indian Town.

On receiving intelligence the 13th instant that a number of persons were assembling on purpose to go to cut off the Indians at Conestogoe I, in concert with Mr. [Thomas] *Forster, the neighbouring magistrate, hurried off an Express with a written message to that party, entreating & beseeching them to desist from such an undertaking, representing to them the cruelty of such an action; that it is barbarous & unchristian in its nature and would be fatal in its consequences to themselves & families; that private persons have no right to take the lives of any under the protection of the Government; that they must, if they proceeded in that affair, lay their accounts to meet with a severe prosecution and become liable even to capital punishment; that they need not expect that the country would endeavour to conceal or screen them from punishment but that they would be detected & given up to the resentment of the Government. These things I urged in the warmest terms in order to prevail with them to drop the enterprise, but without any effect, they pushed on & have actually destroyed some of these Indians, tho how many I have not yet been certainly informed. I nevertheless thought it my duty to give your Honour this timely notice that an action of this nature mayn't be imputed to these frontier Settlements for I know not of one person of prudence or Judgment that has been any wise concerned in it but has been done by some hot headed ill advised persons, & especially by such I imagine as suffered much in their relations by the Ravages committed in the late Indian war.*

John Hay also wrote to Penn. The sheriff had been fashioning his list of the Conestogas' names and possessions on December 27 when the violence at the workhouse interrupted him. He stood aside and let the Rangers kill the Indians, then again took up his pen to tell Penn that fifty or sixty heavily armed men had "rushed into the Town & immediately repaired to the Work House where the Indians were confined, & notwithstanding all opposition of myself and the Coroner, with many others, broke open the Work House, and have killed all the Indians there."

These letters of Shippen, Elder and Hay are the only known surviving accounts written by people closely associated with the incidents of December

1763. They provide slightly different perspectives, but they share a singular theme: no one in Lancaster or Paxton—and especially not the writers themselves—was responsible for or could have prevented what happened.

There is only one other contemporary letter that describes these events. Written not by one of the principal players but by a keen, though hardly neutral, observer, it may be the most revealing. On December 27, David Henderson, a Lancaster Quaker, explained the situation in Lancaster to Joseph Galloway, the Quaker speaker of the Pennsylvania Assembly.

Henderson's writing, like Sheriff Hays's, was interrupted by the massacre of the Indians that afternoon. Unlike Hays or any other writer, Henderson sought not to make excuses for what had occurred but to question why the town's officials had allowed it to occur.

The Indians at Conestoga were killed by fifty-seven men "who are said to be but a small party of that multitude who are enraged ag'st the Residue of the Conestogoe," Henderson reported. The killers were particularly concerned about Will Sock, he said, because he supposedly had "green white scalps in his poss'n since the last breaking out of the Ind'n trouble." But Henderson said he believed this was merely a story invented "to give a Colour to their enterprise."

Henderson said the Conestogas were being held in the Lancaster workhouse

> *at the Risque of their Lives. Because those murderers & their abettors here are so irritated & enraged ag'st those Indians & all others who have avowed their disapprobation of that murder, that none of them are secure from the attempts of that bloodthirsty mob.*
>
> *Rumours & threats of pulling down the Goal & killing the Indians there have been so well attested that the goaler has armed himself & sent off his Child'n. During nights, sundry magistrates have watched with him til an early hour of the morning.*
>
> *I am afraid there is not a good understanding between some of our magistrates & Certain Worthy Representatives of the County, which may have presented measures which might have already been taken to prevent further bloodshed.*

Henderson stopped writing and went about his business. Events that afternoon prompted him to add these lines:

> *The post did not go this morning so the inclosed has not been dispatched till what I feared has come to pass. About 4 hours ago these wild men*

> *came armed (in number 50 or hereabouts) and broke open the Goal in the presence of the Sheriff & Coroner who commanded the peace & did the little in their power to prevent their design tho' in Vain & murdered all the Indians there. They went off hooping and hallowing having rode round the Courthouse in an inglorious triumph discharging their pieces* [& co.].
>
> *The Risque was too great for any of the Inhabitants to interpose. Too many of them approved of the Massacre.*
>
> *They threaten to go to Philad. & murder the Ind's on the Island. They say their Name is Legion. They are Many & will stand by one another. If these Outrages are passed Over with Impunity all Civil Gov't is at an end. I wish better times. God knows where this will end.*

Henderson's letter is notable for indicting not only the Indian killers from Paxton but also their "abettors" in Lancaster. He said that a second raid on the jail had been expected but effective measures had not been taken to thwart it. After what he feared would happen did happen, he said no one in town interfered with the Rangers because "too many of them approved of the massacre."

A well-informed borough Quaker, Henderson probably had reason to dislike these rough Scots-Irish Presbyterian frontiersmen even before they killed the Conestogas. He possibly had a larger ax to grind than he reveals in this letter. But in that hour of calamity, his report seems more reliable than self-protective statements by the officials involved.

CHAPTER 6

"A Mighty Noise and Hubbub"

From late January through the early spring of 1764, Pennsylvanians engaged in an unprecedented debate over current and projected events. Commenting on the actions of the Paxton Boys, dozens of writers produced more than sixty pamphlets—twice as many as had been printed on a variety of subjects in Philadelphia during the previous year. These arguments took the form of essays, dialogues, plays, parodied speeches and scathing satires. All were unsigned, but astute observers soon determined who had written the most significant pieces.

Some pamphleteers attacked the Paxton Boys as Scots-Irish villains who had killed peaceful Indians and threatened the rule of law by marching on Philadelphia. Others targeted Presbyterians, who they believed had goaded the militia into action. On the other side, writers criticized Quakers who opposed military aid for frontier people oppressed by hostile Indians. In addition, they attacked a do-nothing, Quaker-controlled assembly.

The debate also spawned the first real political cartoons in America. Several of these ten cryptic illustrations targeted Benjamin Franklin as friend to Quakers and Indians. One scene depicted a Quaker man ardently seducing an Indian woman. Another showed Quakers and Indians riding on the backs of Scots-Irish and German settlers. Overdrawn and overly wordy by today's standards, the cartoons made an enormous impact on Pennsylvanians who had seen nothing of the kind.

The pamphlets, as verbose and exclamatory as the cartoons, were published, for the most part, in Philadelphia and sold in bookstores, churches

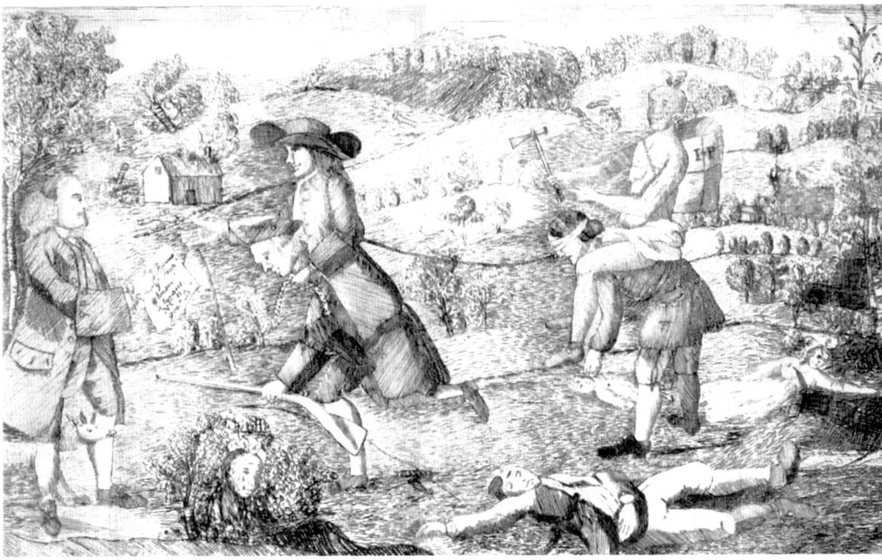

A cartoon drawn during the Paxton uprising shows Benjamin Franklin presiding with the proprietary interests, while Quakers and Indians abuse German and Scots-Irish settlers. *Historical Society of Pennsylvania.*

and taverns throughout the colonies. Each installment was read eagerly and quickly disputed in print by an incensed representative of the other side. Most writers drew stark contrasts between opposing groups: cosmopolitan easterners versus provincial frontiersmen, English versus Scots-Irish, Quakers versus Presbyterians and supporters of the assembly versus backers of the wartime powers of the proprietary governor.

Most of the pamphlets concerned themselves with the threatened attack on the capital and the "Remonstrances" of the Paxton Boys. Fewer fretted over the earlier killing of Indians in Lancaster or the failure of authorities to identify and imprison the killers. Most pamphleteers who mentioned the massacre condemned it, but some condemnations were so qualified by sympathy for the Paxton Boys' grievances that they could have served as model defense summaries at trial.

For example, David James Dove, a Philadelphia schoolmaster who has been credited with writing several pamphlets, maintained in *The Quaker Unmask'd; or, Plain Truth* that the massacre was unlawful. But then he also asked: "Do not Candor, Piety, and Justice require that we should admit of every alleviating Circumstance in [the Paxton Boys'] Favour, rather than take so much Pains (as many do) to aggrivate their Crime and make bad appear worse?" Among several ameliorating circumstances associated with the Conestoga massacre, Dove suggested, were that "none of those killed at Lancaster were by Design kept one Moment in Torment; whereas many of our Frontier Inhabitants have been wantonly kept whole Days and Nights in exquisite Tortures."

The Paxton Boys' defenders wrote the most cutting satirical pieces because they had the broadest target: the presumed hypocrisy of Quakers taking up arms to defend themselves against possible attack in Philadelphia while refusing to provide adequate resources for frontier defense. Further, these writers blasted Quakers for actively supporting the Indians, both by subsidizing the Conestogas as wards of the government and by trading extensively with various tribes. The author of *The Cloven-Foot Discovered*, the sole tract printed on the press of the Ephrata Cloister in Lancaster County, maintained that "In many things change but the Name,/ Quakers and Indians are the same." This author also wrote some of the most derogatory lines in the pamphlets.

Go on good Christians, never spare
To give your Indians Clothes to wear;
Send 'em good Beef, and Pork, and Bread,
Guns, Powder, Flints and store of Lead,
To Shoot your Neighbours through the head.

The Quakers returned their share of blasts against Scots-Irish Presbyterians, or "Piss-brutarians," as one writer termed them. The author of *A Dialogue* created an obnoxious character to brag that the Paxton Boys had accomplished more than many world conquerors: "We have, and it gives me Pleasure to think on't, Slaughter'd, kill'd and cut off a whole Tribe! A Nation at once!"

In *A Looking-Glass for Presbyterians*, the Philadelphia lawyer Isaac Hunt answered Dove's *The Quaker Unmask'd; or, Plain Truth* by warning that the Paxton Boys followed a long line of Scotch Presbyterian rebels who, if given power, would unleash similar violent rebellion on Pennsylvania. Then he mockingly admired their bravery for killing unarmed Indian men, women and children: "The Fame of this noble Exploit ought surely to be recorded in the Annals of America for the Honor of the religious, Christian Presbyterian."[12]

Of all these pamphlets, two anonymous tracts on opposing sides are most often cited. Benjamin Franklin wrote the longest pamphlet to describe and condemn the killing of the Conestogas: *A Narrative of the Late Massacres, in Lancaster County, of a Number of Indians, Friends of this Province, By Persons Unknown. With some Observations on the same.* Lancaster Anglican minister Thomas Barton's *The Conduct of the Paxton-Men, Impartially Represented: with Some Remarks on the Narrative* rebutted Franklin point by point within an elaborate defense of the Paxton Boys' actions in Lancaster.

By all accounts, Franklin fired the first shot in the pamphlet war on or about January 30, 1764. That was about five weeks after the second massacre and nearly a week before the Paxton Boys marched into Germantown, the incident that prompted most of the pamphleteers to take up pens.

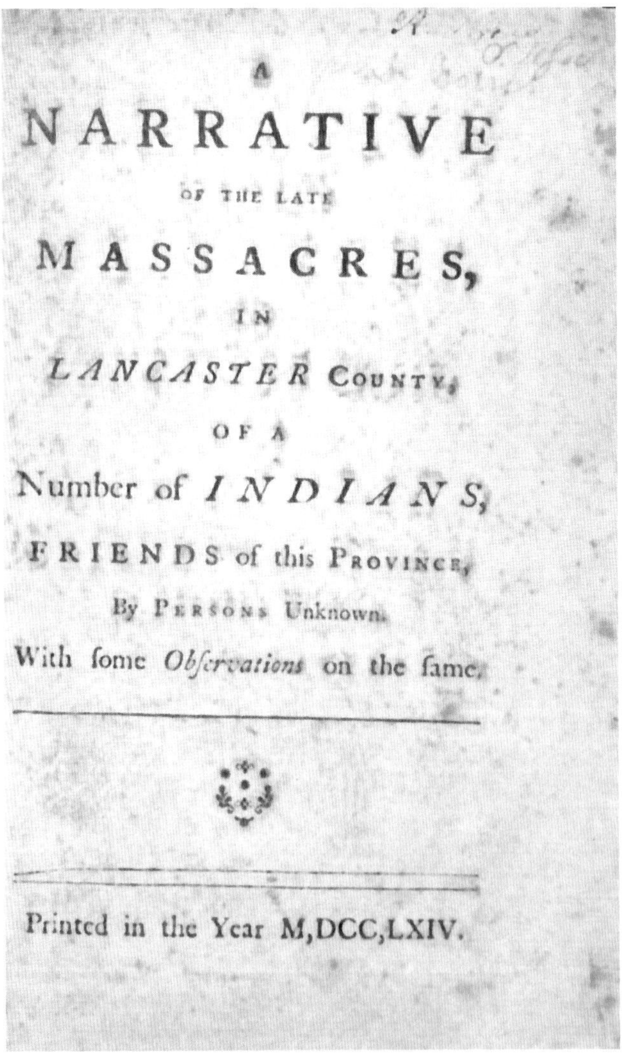

A
NARRATIVE
OF THE LATE
MASSACRES,
IN
LANCASTER COUNTY,
OF A
Number of *INDIANS*,
FRIENDS of this PROVINCE,
By PERSONS Unknown.
With ſome *Obſervations* on the ſame.

Printed in the Year M,DCC,LXIV.

Front cover of Benjamin Franklin's 1764 pamphlet, *A Narrative of the Late Massacres*, which decried the killing of the Conestogas. *Historical Society of Pennsylvania.*

Franklin's writing has become, by far, the most influential. Some historians, particularly in the nineteenth century, accepted Franklin's passionate account of the workhouse slaughter as literal. Helen Hunt Jackson's *A Century of Dishonor* in 1881 quoted it verbatim, without qualification.

Alison Olson argued in a 1999 essay in the *Pennsylvania Magazine of History and Biography* that Franklin's piece is overrated because it was not widely read at the time and provoked few rejoinders. By attracting Thomas Barton's detailed rebuttal alone, however, Franklin did more than any other pamphleteer to assure that both sides of this story would endure.

"It has always been observed, that Indians, settled in the Neighborhood of White People, do not increase, but diminish continually," Franklin began. "This Tribe accordingly went on diminishing, till there remained in their Town on the Manor, but 20 Persons, viz. 7 Men, 5 Women, and 8 Children, Boys and Girls."

Franklin named and provided personal information about ten of the Conestogas. His description of Sally, an older woman whom he called Wyanjoy, but whom John Hay had identified as Tea-wonsha-i-ong, was particularly detailed:

> *A Woman much esteemed by all that knew her, for her prudent and good Behaviour in some very trying Situations of Life. She was a truly good and an amiable Woman, had no Children of her own, but a distant Relation dying, she had taken a Child of that Relation's, to bring up as her own, and performed towards it all the Duties of an affectionate Parent.*[13]

Franklin then described the massacre at Conestoga:

> *Fifty-seven Men, from some of our Frontier Townships, who had projected the Destruction of this little Common-wealth, came, all well-mounted, and armed with Firelocks, Hangers and Hatchets, having travelled through the Country in the Night, to Conestogoe Manor. There they surrounded the small Village of Indian Huts, and just at Break of Day broke into them all at once. Only three Men, two Women, and a young Boy, were found at home, the rest being out among the neighbouring White People, some to sell the Baskets, Brooms and Bowls they manufactured, and others on other Occasions. These poor defenceless Creatures were immediately fired upon, stabbed and hatcheted to Death! The good Shehaes, among the rest, cut to Pieces in his Bed. All of them were scalped, and otherwise horribly mangled. Then their Huts were set on Fire, and most of them burnt down.*

> *When the Troop, pleased with their own Conduct and Bravery, but enraged that any of the poor Indians had escaped the Massacre, rode off, and in small Parties, by different Roads, went home.*

Franklin explained that the surviving Indians were removed to the workhouse, where the "cruel Men" from Paxton attacked them:

> *Fifty of them, armed as before, dismounting, went directly to the Work-house, and by Violence broke open the Door, and entered with the utmost Fury in their Countenances. When the poor Wretches saw they had* no *Protection nigh, nor could possibly escape, and being without the least Weapon for Defence, they divided into their little Families, the Children clinging to the Parents; they fell on their Knees, protested their Innocence, declared their Love to the English, and that, in their whole Lives, they had never done them Injury; and in this Posture they all received the Hatchet! Men, Women and little Children—were every one inhumanly murdered!—in cold Blood…!*

Franklin said that the governor's proclamations and offer of a reward for the killers so far had produced nothing, "the Murderers having given out such Threatenings against those that disapprove their Proceedings, that the whole County seems to be in Terror, and no one durst speak what he knows; even the Letters from thence are unsigned, in which any Dislike is expressed of the Rioters."

Then Franklin went on the attack. He criticized those who claimed the murders were justified because hostile Indians had killed their relatives. "If any Indian injures me," he wrote, "does it follow that I may revenge that Injury on all Indians?" He inferred that killing peaceful Indians because of the acts of hostile Indians was motivated by racial differences because "the only Crime of these poor Wretches seems to have been, that they had a reddish brown Skin, and black Hair."

Franklin spent several pages demolishing another claimed justification for the murders: that the scriptures had commanded Joshua to destroy the Heathen. "Horrid Perversion of Scripture and of Religion!" he wrote, "to father the worst of Crimes on the God of Peace and Love!"

Christians should extend mercy toward strangers, Franklin said, and he provided several examples from history and the classics. But he said the Conestogas "would have been safer among the ancient Heathens, with whom the Rites of Hospitality were *sacred*." In fact, he noted, the Conestogas "would have been safe in any Part of the known World, except in the Neighbourhood of the CHRISTIAN WHITE SAVAGES of Peckstang and Donegall!"

He called on those accusing the Conestogas and Moravian Indians of fraternizing with the enemy to produce evidence against them:

> *Let them satisfy the Public that even Will Soc, the most obnoxious of all that Tribe, was really guilty of those Offences against us which they lay to his Charge. But if he was, ought he not to have been fairly tried? He lived under our Laws, and was subject to them; he was in our Hands, and might easily have been prosecuted; was it* English *Justice to condemn and execute him unheard? Conscious of his own Innocence, he did not endeavour to hide himself when the Door of the Work-house, his Sanctuary, was breaking open;* I will meet them, *says he,* for they are my Brothers. *These Brothers of his shot him down at the Door, while the Word Brothers was still between his Teeth! But if Will Soc was a bad Man, what had poor old Shehaes done? What could he or the other poor old Men and Women do? What had little Boys and Girls done; what could Children of a Year old, Babes at the Breast, what could they do, that they too must be shot and hatcheted? Horrid to relate! and in their Parents Arms! This is done by no civilized Nation in Europe. Do we come to America to learn and practice the Manners of Barbarians?*

Near the end of his writing, Franklin described what he hoped would happen to the "Unmanly Men" who had slaughtered women and children:

> *O ye unhappy Perpetrators of this horrid Wickedness! Reflect a Moment on the Mischief ye have done, the Disgrace ye have brought on your Country, on your Religion, and your Bible, on your Families and Children! Think on… the infamous Death that hangs over your Heads. For JUSTICE, though, slow, will come at last. All good People every where detest your Actions. You have imbrued your Hands in innocent Blood; how will you make them clean? The dying Shrieks and Groans of the Murdered, will often sound in your Ears: Their Spectres will sometimes attend you, and affright even your innocent Children! Fly where you will, your Consciences will go with you: Talking in your Sleep shall betray you, in the Delirium of a Fever you yourselves shall make your own Wickedness known.*

Franklin's emotional outburst acutely reflects the indignation felt by pacifist observers of these events, but his projection of the fate of the Paxton

Rangers could not have been more wrong. Some of the killers might have suffered in their own private hell, but none endured an "infamous Death." Infamy requires notoriety, absent because none of the killers has ever been conclusively identified.

On March 17, some six weeks after the *Narrative* appeared, Thomas Barton released his lengthy reply. Printed in Philadelphia by Andrew Steuart, the tract would be sold in Philadelphia, as well as at the shop of John Creaig and elsewhere in Lancaster. The Anglican minister wrote as a "GENTLEMAN in one of the back-Countries to a FRIEND in Philadelphia" and designed his ponderous title and subtitle to cover every aspect of the tract:

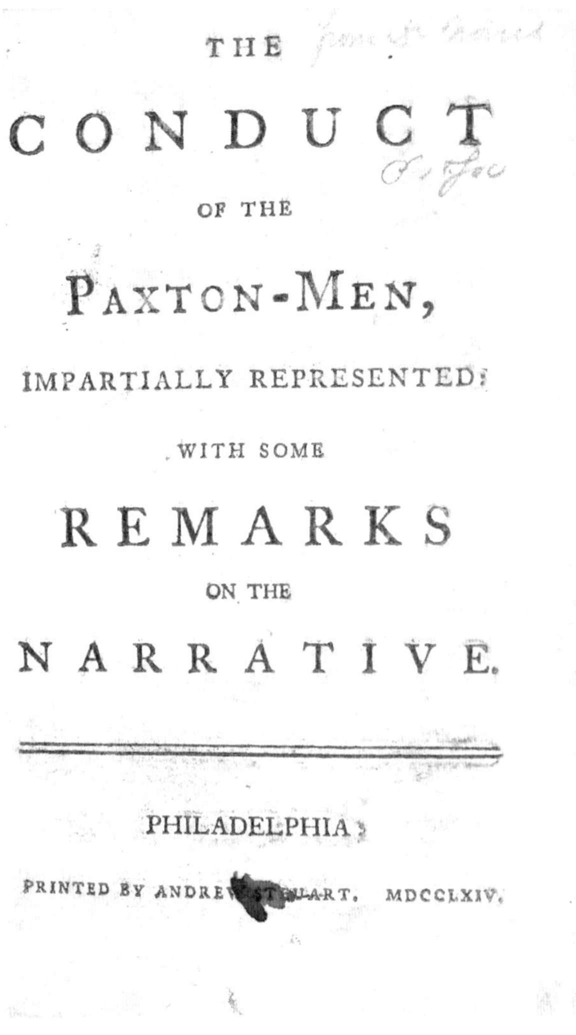
THE

CONDUCT

OF THE

PAXTON-MEN,

IMPARTIALLY REPRESENTED:

WITH SOME

REMARKS

ON THE

NARRATIVE.

PHILADELPHIA:

PRINTED BY ANDREW STEUART. MDCCLXIV.

Front cover of Thomas Barton's 1764 pamphlet, *The Conduct of the Paxton-Men*, which defended the Paxton Boys. *Historical Society of Pennsylvania.*

> *The Conduct of the Paxton-Men, Impartially represented; The Distresses of the Frontiers, and the Complaints and Sufferings of the People fully stated; and the Methods recommended by the wisest Nations, in such Cases, seriously consider'd. With some Remarks upon the Narrative, of the Indian-Massacre, lately publish'd. Interpers'd with several interesting Anecdotes, relating to the Military Genius, and Warlike Principles of the People call'd Quakers: Together-with proper Reflection and Advice upon the whole.*

Barton began by restating the frontiersmen's complaints, which he claimed were supported by nine-tenths of the residents of rural counties. He said the Quakers had maintained and protected the Conestogas ("a Pack of villainous, faithless Savages") and the Moravian Indians ("treacherous, faithless, rascally Indians, some of which can be proved to be Murderers") at the expense of their countrymen on the frontier. So, he asked, "Who is it that has made them Rioters, and then Reproaches, and desires that they may be Shot or Hang'd for being so?"

Then Barton directly attacked Franklin's *Narrative*:

> *A mighty Noise and Hubbub has been made about killing a few Indians In Lancaster-County; and even* Philosophers *and* Legislators *have been employed to raise the Holloo upon those that killed them; and to ransack* Tomes *and Systems, Writers ancient and modern, for Proofs of their Guilt and Condemnation! And what have they proved at last? Why, that the* WHITE SAVAGES *of* Paxton *and* Donegall *have violated the Laws of Hospitality! I can sincerely assure the ingenious and worthy Author of the* NARRATIVE, *that a Shock of* Electricity *would have had a much more sensible Effect upon these People than all the Arguments and Quotations he has produced.*

Barton said he abhorred the massacre, especially of women and children, but imagined that the killers thought it best to slaughter everyone "lest out of the SERPENT'S EGG, there should come a COCKATRICE, and his Fruit should be a fiery flying SERPENT."

The minister continued:

> *Now I have been frequently inform'd. for many Years, by sundry of their nearest Neighbours in the* Conestogoe Manner, *that they were a* drunken, debauch'd, insolent, quarrelsome *Crew; and that ever since the Commencement of the War, they have been a Trouble and Terror*

> *to all around them—as for* Will Soc *and his Brother, I am told there are undoubted Proofs of their Guilt and Treachery—That they have threatened and drawn their Knives upon People who have refused to comply with their Demands, is a Fact well known to Hundreds.*

Barton claimed Lancaster's magistrates wanted to avoid this confrontation by moving the Conestogas to Philadelphia. He said it was not their fault that armed men broke into an unguarded workhouse and killed the occupants:

> *For it seems the Affair was accomplish'd so unexpectedly and suddenly, that not one Half of the Magistrates knew any Thing of the Matter till they were all kill'd; and those that did, could do nothing, unless, it was to go at the Peril of their Lives, among an enraged and armed Multitude, and attack them with* Stones *and* Brickbats.

Barton wondered how Franklin could have known that the Indians "divided into their little Families, their Children clinging to their Parents" before they were killed.

> *This was cruel indeed, if it was so—But I would be glad to know who could give this Gentleman so very particular an Account—I have been told, that not a single Circumstance happened which could have given rise to it; and that the above Story was pick'd up from among a Parcel of old Papers in a* Hop-Garden *or a* Hempfield *(I forget which) upon* Susquehanna.[14]*—And indeed this seems most likely to have been the Case:—For who could possibly tell what pass'd, or how these Indians behaved in the short Interval between their being attacked and all killed, which is said not to have been above Two Minutes. No one had any Kind of Intercourse with them, nor even saw them during that Time, except those that killed them, and they declare, that not one of them appeared in that Posture, nor spoke a Word; and that if they had, it would have been impossible to have heard them for the Noise of the shouting of the Multitude.*

Barton next took issue with Franklin's description of the death of the Conestogas as "murder" at the hands of men who felt commanded by the Bible to "destroy the Heathen." The minister asked how the pamphlet writer had determined that the attack on the Indians was murder: "I should be glad to know, who appointed him a Judge or Jury upon this Affair? Does he find that the Government has call'd it Murder in either of the Proclamations he has quoted?"

The minister also contradicted Franklin's tract on the point of whether the government was pledged to protect the Conestogas:

> *Now whatever might have been the Behaviour of these Indians to the first Settlers of* Pennsylvania, *it is notorious that their Conduct of late has been such, as could give them no Manner of Claim to the Faith, Friendship, or Protection of this Government—That they have been Spies upon all our Actions—have treacherously held a Correspondence with our* avowed *enemies—and have often lent a helping Hand to bring Ruin and desolation upon the Province—and yet to such Wretches as these, it seems we ow'd Protection!—and it was* Murder *to put them to Death!*

Barton then answered Franklin's charge that killing the Indians was un-Christian and inhospitable by presenting his own examples from history and the Bible to show that "those in the first Rank of Glory…have resisted, destroy'd or expelled *Traitors* and *Tyrants*, the *Pests*, the *Burthens*, and the *Butchers* of Mankind."

He concluded by advising Quakers who had befriended Indians, and thereby aided the enemy, to heed the Paxton Rangers' message: "Instead of yoking themselves to CANNON, and dragging them along to defend BARRACKS, and fight WIND-MILLS, they [should] suffer the Complaints of the People to be heard, their Grievances redress'd, and their Country rescued from total Ruin."

Barton and Franklin both ended their pamphlets with the type of rhetorical flourishes popular at the time and prevalent in most of the other tracts that make up the Paxton pamphlets. The partisan and passionate nature of the tracts added more heat than light to a still-volatile situation.

CHAPTER 7

"Shot—Scalped—Hacked—and Cut to Pieces"

The debate in Lancaster and Philadelphia over why the Conestogas had been massacred and who was most responsible continued long after publication of the Paxton pamphlets. Some observers believed nothing could excuse a slaughter of defenseless Indians under government protection. Others believed the Conestogas had invited their own deaths by acting as spies for hostile Indians. Still others held a soft middle ground, condemning the murders while professing to understand the murderers' motivations.

In the first weeks, months and years after the massacre, thoughtful observers also wondered whether Lancaster's ministers, magistrates and other leaders had been complicitous. Given the obvious danger the unsatisfied Paxton Rangers posed to the remaining Conestogas after the attack on Indian Town, these critics asked: Why didn't county officials place a more secure guard around the workhouse? Why didn't someone try to stop the killers before they left town? And why didn't anyone seriously pursue identification of suspects so the guilty could be arrested and tried?

Some early historians, especially Quakers, placed as much or more emphasis on the flaccid response of the Lancaster community to the murders as on the murderers themselves. As time passed and new generations lost touch with the nuances of the situation, however, these concerns faded away.

Most of the early commentators echoed Franklin's *Narrative* or otherwise condemned the Paxtonians. Many of these first shots came from Quaker and Moravian historians, writers who needed no encouragement to condemn Scots-Irish Presbyterians generally and the Paxton Rangers specifically.

One of the first outsiders' accounts of the Paxton Rangers' assault on the Lancaster workhouse came from an exceptional source. Charles Mason temporarily abandoned his survey with Jeremiah Dixon of the boundary between Pennsylvania and Maryland and traveled to Lancaster in January 1765. He said he planned to quench his "curiosity to see the place where was perpetrated last Winter the Horrid and inhuman murder" of the Conestogas.

Mason's primary concern was not the killers but the town's passive response to the Rangers' invasion, as he clarified in his field record: "Strange it was that the Town though as large as most Market Towns in England, never offered to oppose [the Rangers], though its more than probable they on request might have been assisted by a Company of his Majesties Troops who were then in the Town…no honor to them!"

The surveyor added in his brief account that evidence the Conestogas had been dealing with hostile Indians "could never be proved against the men and women and children (some in their Mothers' wombs that never saw light)."[15]

The Moravian minister and historian George Henry Loskiel was first to mention the Conestoga massacre in a book. His *History of the Mission of the United Brethren among the Indians in North America* was published in Saxony in 1789 and in the United States in 1794, three decades after the massacre.

Practically bound to take up the cause of the Moravian Indians and the beleaguered Conestogas to their south, Loskiel bluntly condemned the Paxton Rangers as "barbarians (who) cruelly murdered them all, throwing their mangled bodies into the street." Despite this bold crime, Loskiel asserted, "it soon became evident, that an incredible number of persons, and even many of the inhabitants of Philadelphia, were in a secret connection with the ring leaders, and people in general showed so little respect for Government at that time, that none were taken up, though they walked publicly in the streets."

Robert Proud was the first general historian to discuss the massacre. Although he published *The History of Pennsylvania in North America* in 1798, he wrote most of his book in the late 1770s, just a decade and a half following the event. A lifelong Quaker, Proud relied heavily on Franklin's *Narrative* and also developed his own interpretation of what had happened, which influenced generations of historians.

Proud condemned Presbyterian ministers for arousing the Paxton Rangers. "Certain most furious zealots, among the preachers of a numerous sect," inspired the Rangers to action, he wrote. These ministers used the "pretense of religion to cover their barbarity."

Proud called the Rangers themselves "*armed demi-savages,* inhabitants of Lancaster county, principally from the townships of Paxtang and

Donnegal" who "committed the most horrible massacre, that ever was heard of in this, or perhaps any other province, with impunity! And under the notion of extirpating the Heathen from the earth, as Joshua did of old, that these saints might possess the land alone, they murdered the remains of a whole tribe."

Proud echoed Franklin's description of the assault on the workhouse and took a shot at Lancaster's magistrates:

> *The bloody scene was completed in the town of Lancaster itself; where the remainder of the tribe, which had escaped the first slaughter, taking refuge, declaring their innocence, and crying for mercy and protection, were through the connivance, if not the encouragement, of the Christian-professing Magistrates, and other principal persons of that town, all inhumanly butchered, in cold blood, even infants at the breast, by the same party of armed ruffians, at mid-day, without opposition, or the least molestation!—to the lasting infamy of the inhabitants of that place, who had power sufficient to prevent it!*

In the spring of 1806, Robert Sutliff, a British Quaker merchant, traveled through Lancaster and commented at some length on the massacre in the workhouse. He drew liberally from Franklin and/or Proud in describing an incident that he believed had been provoked by "a number of people, actuated by the wildest religious enthusiasm, in which they were encouraged by some furious zealots among their preachers."

Like Loskiel, the Moravian missionary John Heckewelder mentioned the massacre in several books describing Indian life. He fully sympathized with the plight of all Indians, once stating, "I felt ashamed of being a *white man*."

In *History, Manners, and Customs of the Indian Nations Who Once Inhabited Pennsylvania and the Neighboring States*, published in 1819, Heckewelder explained how the 1763 massacre had poisoned the treaty of the previous year at Lancaster. He quoted an Indian as saying that the Conestogas' blood had extinguished the council fire from that treaty, so that "not one spark was left us whereby to kindle a new fire." Heckewelder also quoted Indians as making a more damaging claim by distinguishing "between a *warrior* and a *murderer*" and determining that those who had killed the Conestogas were cowards.

In 1820, Heckewelder published for the first time a graphic account of the workhouse slaughter by William Henry Jr. in his *Narrative of the Mission of the United Brethren among the Delaware and Mohegan Indians from its Commencement, in the Year 1740, to the Close of the Year 1808.*

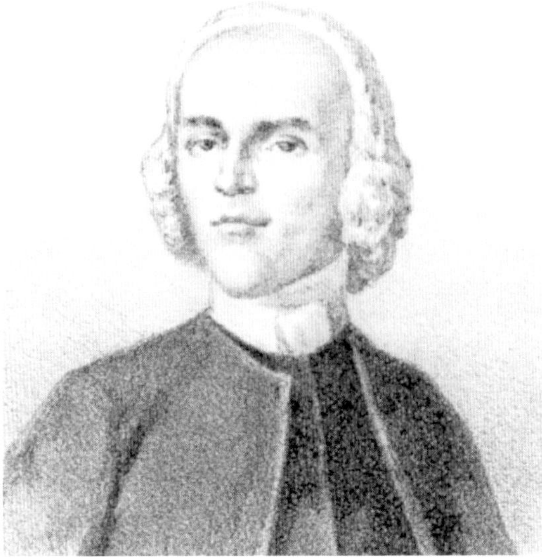

Lancaster gunsmith and inventor William Henry. His son, William Henry Jr., wrote the only eyewitness account of the aftermath of the massacre in Lancaster's workhouse. *Lancaster County Historical Society.*

Of some two thousand residents of Lancaster Borough in 1763, not one recorded the scene in the workhouse yard at the time of the massacre. At least no such record survives. But gunmaker and inventor William Henry's son, six years old in 1763, described the dead bodies fifty-seven years later. The young boy was at his father's home, near the county courthouse on Centre Square, when the massacre occurred. He and other boys followed people running down King Street toward the commotion at the workhouse. He recalled watching the Rangers hastily leave the scene before he walked into the yard.

Unless he had a photographic memory, it is unlikely that William Henry Jr. remembered all of these details perfectly. After six decades, he may have exaggerated the brutality. (In fact, he noted twice that one Indian's hands had been cut off.) But his strongest images—brains splashed against the workhouse wall, for example—seem to have been seared into his own mind. This is what Henry said he found in the workhouse yard on the afternoon of December 27, 1763:

> *Near the back door of the prison, lay an old Indian and his squaw (wife) particularly well known and esteemed by the people of the town, on account of his placid and friendly conduct. His name was Will Sock; across him and his squaw lay two children, of about the age of three years, whose*

heads were split with the tomahawk, and their scalps all taken off. Toward the middle of the gaol yard, along the west side of the wall, lay a stout Indian, whom I particularly noticed to have been shot in the breast, his legs were chopped with the tomahawk, his hands cut off, and finally a rifle ball discharged in his mouth; so that his head was blown to atoms, and the brains were splashed against, and yet hanging to the wall, for three or four feet around. This man's hands and feet had also been chopped off with a tomahawk. In this manner lay the whole of them, men, women and children, spread about the prison yard: shot—scalped—hacked—and cut to pieces.

Reprinted countless times since 1820, Henry's brief description has joined Franklin's as the most familiar representations of the massacre. For shock value, it has no equal.

In his influential *History of Pennsylvania* (1829), the Philadelphian Thomas F. Gordon made arguments on both sides. He acknowledged that some Indians residing within European settlements probably provided information to hostile Indians. But he also censured the Paxton Rangers for planning to kill the Conestogas with "a spirit not less savage than that of the ruthless aborigines." And Gordon criticized Lancaster's magistrates:

It is not possible to exculpate the magistrates of the town from the charge of criminal negligence, since it was in their power to have prevented this assassination, or to have arrested the perpetrators. Captain Robinson [sic], *with a company of highlanders, on their way from Pittsburg, being then at Lancaster, put himself in the way to receive the commands of the civil authority, which made no effort to use the force thus offered it.*

In February 1832, *Hazard's Register of Pennsylvania* published a description of the massacre that would have almost as much impact on subsequent generations of historians as William Henry Jr.'s letter of 1820. Rhoda Barber was the daughter of Robert Barber Jr., one of the three Quaker founders of Wright's Ferry and the man who unwittingly hosted some of the Paxton Rangers following the massacre at Conestoga. Born three years after the massacre, she received her stories from her parents and two older brothers and wrote them down in an old school journal when she was sixty-four, a year older than Henry when he set his memories to paper.

Barber titled this collection *Recollections Written in 1830 of Life in Lancaster County 1726–1782 and a History of Settlement at Wright's Ferry, on Susquehanna River*. Her account of the massacre is by far the most colorful of her reminiscences.

Although written from secondhand knowledge more than half a century after the events occurred, Barber's memoir commands attention because of its unusual details: an Indian child's toy gun tied to a Ranger's saddle, for example, and burned Indian bodies looking like "half-consum'd logs."

The Barbers were close friends with the Conestogas. "My older brother and sisters us'd to be whole days with [the Indians]," Barber wrote. "They were great beggars and the children were so attached to them they could not bear to hear them refus'd any thing they asked for."[16] The writer was wholly sympathetic to the Conestogas' plight, which surely colored some of her memories.

This excerpt comes from Barber's simple journal book, preserved in the collections of the Historical Society of Pennsylvania.

> [On] *a very cold morning in the 12 mo 1763 a German neighbour came to my fathers house requesting him to go with him in pursuit of some who had been at his house the preceding night whom he termed robber they had behaved in a very disorderly manner such as melting the pewter on the stove and other things of the same kind, my father supposing it had been some persons in a frolick advis'd him to take no notice of it—he was scarcly gone when five or six men came in, they had guns which they left outside, they were very cold, their coats cover'd with snow and sleet. I don't think my father was personaly acquainted with any of them tho he knew from what part of the country they came, he made up the fire to warm them, and according to the hospitality of the times treated them with the customary morning refreshments while they warm'd themselves they enquir'd why the Indians were suffer'd to live peaceably here, my father told them they were quite inoffensive living on their own land and injuring no one, they ask'd what would be the consequences were they destroy'd, my father told them he thought they would be as liable to punishment as if they had destroy'd so many whites, they were of a different opinion at length they went away without telling what they had been about, in the mean time my two brothers ten and twelve years old had been out looking at the strangers horses (as such boys are wont to do) which were hitched in a waggon shed which stood near the door, after they were gone my brothers said they had tomahawks tyed to their saddles and they were bloody, that they also had Christies gun (Christie was a little Indian boy about the age of my brothers, they were much attach'd to him, he was their playmate in all their sports, made their bows and arrows and was indeed as a brother*[17]*) while they wondered what it could mean a messenger came from Hare* [a German neighbor who

> served as an Indian caretaker] *giving information of the dreadfull deed, my father and some others went down to see them buried, shocking indeed was the sight, the dead bodies lay among the rubbish of their burnt cabbins like half consum'd logs.*

Barber briefly described the second massacre. She said it might have been averted if the magistrates had accepted Captain Robertson's offer of assistance,

> *but the magistrates could not be found 'tho it was done by day light whether through fear or that they conniv'd at it was never known, their excuses seem'd too trifling to be admitted, one could not find his wig and things of as little consequence were pleaded by others, an Episcopalian minister in Lancaster wrote to vindicate them bringing scripture to prove that it was right to destroy the heathen and very many were of the same opinion.*

The next published reference to the massacre, in James Wimer's *Events in Indian History* (1842), drew most of its material from Proud, Franklin, Heckewelder and Henry. Wimer included one original item: a lithograph, dated 1841, depicting the Paxton Rangers killing the Conestogas in front of the Lancaster Prison. The Paxtonians are dressed in nineteenth-century formal attire, including top hats, while the Indians they are about to slaughter are half naked in December. This sole depiction of the massacre has been reproduced repeatedly, usually without reference to its inaccuracies.

But Wimer's rehashed history and anachronistic illustration were not the most objectionable renderings of the Conestoga massacre in the 1840s. In the summer of 1843, a prominent Lancaster County attorney and amateur historian forged what proved to be an exceedingly successful effort to rehabilitate the Paxton Rangers.

CHAPTER 8

"One of Those Youthful Ebullitions of Wrath"

Redmond Conyngham spent the spring and summer of his sixty-second year diligently distorting the story of the Conestoga massacre. He tampered with evidence; he fabricated documents; he boldly lied; and he designed an 1843 series of newspaper articles in the *Lancaster Intelligencer & Journal* to persuade readers that earlier accounts had misrepresented the Paxton Rangers. He achieved a major bonus by successfully hoodwinking generations of historians.

Born at Philadelphia in 1781, Conyngham moved to Luzerne County as a young adult and represented Luzerne and neighboring counties in the state Senate in the early 1820s. From Luzerne, he went on to Carlisle, Cumberland County, and then to Paradise, Lancaster County, where he spent the rest of his life practicing law and writing and speaking about historical subjects. He died in 1846.

Conyngham had first-rate credentials. A graduate of Princeton College and trustee of Dickinson College, he frequently wrote about early Lancaster and Pennsylvania history, especially local and regional Indian history. He contributed to the respected publications of the Historical Society of Pennsylvania and the American Philosophical Society. A contemporary called Conyngham a "finished scholar."

Conyngham became a serious serial fabricator when he reached midlife, creating new documents at least as early as 1829. In a 1962 article for *Pennsylvania History* magazine, William Hunter, chief of the research and publication division of the Pennsylvania Historical and Museum Commission, described Conyngham's fabrication of at least eight items. These materials were grouped as "Provincial Correspondence: 1750 to 1765" in *Hazard's Register* of December 19, 1829. Samuel Hazard, an amateur historian himself and curator of the Historical Society of Pennsylvania, published the texts without identifying the contributor.

Hunter found that the eight fabricated letters share multiple failings. Though supposedly penned by several individuals, they exhibit a similar writing style; they tend to romanticize facts; they are vaguely identified as to date, place, writer and recipient; and they contain blatant factual errors.

Sherman Day, among other historians of the 1830s and 1840s, quoted from these fraudulent texts. In his *Historical Collections of the State of Pennsylvania* (1843), Day attributed the "Provincial Correspondence" to "Mr. Conyngham's notes."

These fabrications continue to plague historians, Hunter noted: "Originating as substitutes for history and owing their first acceptance to the general unavailability of authentic records, the fraudulent texts have in fact survived in uneasy coexistence with the genuine documents and sometimes even in opposition to them."

Hunter focused on the "Provincial Correspondence," but that fraud has considerable company. Historian Charles Hanna, who examined an enormous number of sources while researching *The Wilderness Trail* (1911), decided that Conyngham had "invented most of his facts and distorted the rest."

This would include Conyngham's contributions to the *Intelligencer & Journal*. The weekly newspaper printed the historian's stories about early Lancaster County history on fifteen of its front pages between March 28 and August 22, 1843. The writer laid a fairly factual foundation for the county's history before building his faulty framework for the Paxton Rangers. So most readers probably went along with his take on the massacre as he designed virtually everything he wrote to rehabilitate the Rangers and dig the Indians' graves deeper.

Historical Sketches, Containing Facts Not Generally Known—the overall title of Conyngham's series—fit the articles perfectly: this version of events was not generally known because it had not existed before. As with the "Provincial Correspondence: 1750 to 1765," Conyngham took advantage of a dearth of authentic records to create inauthentic ones.

Unlike early Quaker historians, who exhibited a strong bias for helpless Indians and against bloodthirsty Rangers, Conyngham went beyond bias to burden the record with a fiction about faultless Rangers and mendacious Indians.

The historian George W. Franz identified six "suspicious documents" he believed Conyngham had fabricated in the *Intelligencer* series. Franz listed these documents, without much elaboration, in *Paxton, a Study of Community Structure and Mobility in the Colonial Pennsylvania Backcountry* (1989). He warned historians to stay away from the documents and named published authors who had relied on them.

Like the letters Conyngham had created in Carlisle, several of the *Intelligencer* items were dated only by year, at most. Conyngham claimed the materials were "in my possession."

In two letters, Shippen and Elder asked Governor James Hamilton to move the Conestogas to Philadelphia for their safety.[18] The supposed Shippen letter simply does not exist. Conyngham dated the purported Elder letter precisely: September 13, 1763. The actual letter of that date, in the archives of the Dauphin County Historical Society, is similar in many respects, but it says nothing about moving the Conestogas. Elder urged that course in another letter.

Conyngham also published a letter that he claimed Elder had sent to Colonel James Burd in 1765, although no remaining Elder letters postdate 1764. All the Rangers desired, the letter claimed, was a fair trial in Lancaster. This letter also said the Rangers shot the Indians but used no edged weapons. "The inference is plain," Elder supposedly wrote, "that the *bodies* of the Indians were thus *mangled* after death by certain *persons*, to excite a feeling against the *Paxton Boys*."

The ideas planted in these letters—that Shippen wanted to protect the Conestogas by moving them to Philadelphia and that the Paxton Rangers did not abuse the Indians and would have been delighted to defend themselves at trial—had a clear object: to reduce the culpability of the Rangers and Lancaster authorities.

Far more serious are the fabricated narratives of Matthew Smith and Lazarus Stewart describing the massacres at Conestoga and the Lancaster workhouse. These fake reminiscences have marred retellings of the story to the present day.

Conyngham claimed that "Smith's Narrative" had been "communicated by a father to his son, in Carlisle, and by that gentleman to the writer." Although no one previously had suggested that one of the leading negotiators at Germantown had ridden with the murderers in Lancaster County, Conyngham had Smith admit to being one of the "chief actors in the destruction."

According to this undated account, Smith rode to Conestoga the night before the massacre. "I saw Indians armed," he claimed. "They were strangers; they outnumbered us by dozens." According to the fabricated letter, Smith summoned reinforcements and, on the morning of December 14, "the moment we were perceived an Indian fired at us, and rushed forward brandishing his tomahawk. Tom cried 'mark him,' and he fell by more than one ball; ______ ran up and cried out, 'it is the villain who murdered my mother.' This speech roused to vengeance, and Conestogue lay harmless before us."

Here Conyngham's Smith claimed the village contained not six Conestogas but several dozen armed "strangers," that is, unknown and therefore likely hostile Indians. He said one of the Indians had murdered a Ranger's mother, although he withheld that man's name. Most important, he said an Indian attacked the raiding party, thus implying that the Rangers fired in self-defense.

In this fake letter, when Smith discovered that some Indians had escaped the slaughter and were housed in the Lancaster workhouse, he joined Stewart and others to finish the job. Conyngham's Smith claimed the plan was to capture an Indian "assassin" of another unnamed Ranger's mother. The letter said that Elder opposed this idea and suggested appealing to Pennsylvania officials, to no avail. The Rangers rode to Lancaster. A small number of men entered the workhouse. They killed everyone. The fictional letter claimed that the Rangers recognized two of the dead Indians as murderers. "This gave quiet to the frontiers," Smith concluded, "for no murder of our defenseless inhabitants has since happened."

And so Conyngham absolved Elder of guilt, justified the killings by claiming murderers were among the murdered and attributed frontier peace to the Lancaster slaughter.

In Stewart's "Declaration," allegedly written in 1777, the year before Stewart died, Ranger scouts traced the unidentified "murderer" back to the village and demanded that he be turned over. However, "the Indians assumed a warlike attitude, tomahawks were raised and the firearms glistened in the sun; shots were fired upon the scouts, who went back for additional force. They returned and you know the event—Conestogue was reduced to ashes." Thus Conyngham's Stewart placed even more responsibility than Conyngham's Smith on the Conestogas themselves because they refused to turn over the "murderer" and assumed a "warlike attitude."

In this fabricated letter, Stewart went on to say that the "murderer" the Rangers were looking for escaped the slaughter at Conestoga. He claimed that "the friendly and unfriendly were placed in the Workhouse at Lancaster" as an explanation for why all of the Indians had to be killed. "What could secure them from the vengeance of an exasperated people?" the false Stewart asked. "The doors were forced and the hapless Indians perished."

In possibly his most creative fabrication, Conyngham produced a courtroom dialogue for the keeper of the jail and workhouse, Felix Donnally. Contrary to Sheriff John Hay's claim that Hay and Matthias Slough alone were at the workhouse when the Rangers arrived, Donnally's fake deposition claimed that he and Slough could do nothing to stop the enraged Rangers. Conyngham's Donnally said:

> *The breaking open of the door alarmed me; armed men broke in; they demanded the* strange Indian *to be given up; they run by me; the Indians guessed their intention; they seized billets of wood from the pile; but the* three *most active were shot; others came to their assistance; I was stupefied before I could shake off my surprise; the Indians were killed and their murderers away.*

The deposition continued in dialogue form, with no indication of who asked the questions:

"Question—'You say, "Indians armed themselves with wood;" did those Indians attack the rioters?'"

"Answer—'They did. If they had not been shot, they would have killed the men who entered, for they were the strongest.'"

So Conyngham's Donnally, "stupefied" by the murder of fourteen people within his sight, also asserted that the Rangers shot the Conestogas in self-defense. This time the aggressor Indians were armed with lethal chunks of firewood.

There are other fabricated documents besides the six letters George Franz identified. Several seek to exonerate Elder. For example, on May 9, Conyngham presented a fragment of a letter, with no date or identification of author. "The Rev. Mr. Elder rode after the Paxton Boys to keep them from going to Lancaster, when they threatened to shoot his horse," the letter said. Later in the series, Conyngham elaborated on this incident: "Mr. Elder rode up in front and said, 'As your pastor, I command you to relinquish your design.' 'Give way then,' said one Smith, 'or your horse dies,' presenting his rifle. To save his horse, to which he was much attached Mr. E. drew him aside, and the Rangers were off on their fatal errand."

In actuality, the only time Elder himself addressed this matter, in his December 16, 1763 letter to John Penn, the minister said he sent a messenger after the Rangers in an effort to stop them.[19]

In addition to creating these and other letters, Conyngham made statements in his narrative that he must have known to be false.

In the June 10 installment, Conyngham repudiated much of Franklin's *Narrative*. For example, based on Franklin's description of only ten of the twenty Conestogas, Conyngham implied that most of the Conestogas were grown men. It is transparently deceitful to count only the one child and three women Franklin named among his ten subjects and pretend that the other sixteen Conestogas were men. Conyngham surely knew that Sheriff Hay had sent a list of the names and relationships of the Conestogas to Governor Penn. Based on information provided by two of the Conestoga women, Hay identified seven men, five women and eight "boys" or "girls" by name and relationship. There is no authentic challenge to that list.[20]

Half-truths or whole fabrications season much of the newspaper series, but they are particularly pungent in the May 23 installment. Conyngham provided a narrative account of what happened in December 1763. This exercise included both adopting other people's words as his own and putting his words into other people's mouths.

The writer quickly passed over the events of December 14 to discuss December 27 in detail. He claimed that "about twenty" Rangers rode to the Lancaster workhouse seeking one Indian known to be a murderer. Their signal to enter the town, Conyngham emphasized, was the last tolling of the bell calling parishioners to the delayed Christmas service at the Anglican church.[21]

Conyngham claimed that if the "chivalrous character of Stewart and his faithful Rangers" had prevailed, only one Indian would have been taken from the workhouse. But "three of the oldest" among the group took over and killed the Conestogas as they tried to escape. Still Conyngham emphasized, "No children were killed by the Paxton Boys. No act of Savage Butchery was committed."

Conyngham said the Rangers struck while the magistrates were in church: "no blame can attach to them." The fault, he claimed, was Captain James Robertson's. According to Conyngham, when Robertson was asked to help protect the Indians with his troops, he replied, "Indians are dogs who prowl in the night, the sooner they are knocked in the head the better; I shall not move one step unless ordered by General Gage."

Conyngham concluded by claiming that the Indians, seeing their danger, "seized such missiles as were near…the assailants fired, and their shots proved fatal."

This account is entirely fictional. Before 1843, no one had suggested that as few as twenty Rangers had participated in the December 27 attack; no one (except Chief Magistrate Shippen) had defended the magistrates with such conviction; no one had exonerated Stewart or attacked Robertson (or fabricated Robertson's speech) with such abandon; no one had attempted to justify the death of the Indians by claiming they tried to defend themselves; and no one had pretended that the Rangers did not kill children.

Nor had anyone praised the Rangers with such bold enthusiasm before these newspaper articles. Conyngham had introduced and romanticized his favorite band of warriors in the April 25 installment: "The Rangers were composed of Hunters, men capable of enduring fatigue, and in character bold, resolute and enterprising…Their peculiar talents were fitted for the times in which they lived. Those times have passed away, and with them the Rangers of those days *have* also disappeared."

On the Fourth of July, Conyngham wrote: "Truth is sacred, immutable, and inviolate. Error is created by circumstances, and prejudices." Why would a man make such a statement and then attempt to rehabilitate the Paxton Rangers and Lancaster's magistrates by deliberately erring? Two biographical details provide cause for speculation.

As a boy, Conyngham lived in the County of Donegal, Ireland, for several years. He certainly established some allegiance to the Irish, an allegiance no doubt solidified when his Irish grandfather willed him £2,000 a year. Already practiced at fabricating documents by 1843, Conyngham may have needed no other nudge to create a more positive record for the Scots-Irish Rangers than his own Irish blood and an editor's offer of ample space.

His defense of the magistrates may have been prompted by his wife's family ties. Elizabeth Yeates Conyngham was Edward Shippen's great-granddaughter. Conyngham may have felt a need to fashion excuses for the magistrates to uphold the Shippen family's honor—perhaps especially in light of the fact that one of Shippen's granddaughters married the most famous traitor in American history. Elizabeth Conyngham and Peggy Shippen, wife of Benedict Arnold, were cousins.

Whatever his motivation, Conyngham severely warped the massacre story. Sherman Day republished these fabrications later in 1843. Subsequent Paxton apologists enthusiastically picked up Conyngham's torch.

In a lengthy address to the Historical Society of Pennsylvania in the spring of 1860, Benjamin J. Wallace, editor of *The Presbyterian Quarterly Review*, praised the Scots-Irish and denigrated the American Indian. In defending the Paxton Rangers and Lancaster County's officials, he drew much of his argument from Conyngham's fake Smith and Stewart letters, and he defended Edward Shippen, John Elder, John Harris and the Paxton Rangers largely on the basis of other fabricated letters. Although he admitted he would not justify the events of December 1763, Wallace added, "we are, for the truth of history, to distinguish them from murder and individual crime."

For the truth of history, it should be noted that Wallace was a member of Elder's church and a descendant of John Harris. He had a divinity degree from Princeton, the Presbyterian university that Shippen had helped found and from which Conyngham had graduated. Wallace had a reputation as a first-rate clergyman, professor and editor; but he also was a front-pew, partisan, Scots-Irish Presbyterian.

Redmond Conyngham's most influential acolyte was William Henry Egle (1833–1901), a prominent Harrisburg physician, historian and genealogist. Egle organized Dauphin County's medical society, presided over the county's historical society and toiled as the state librarian. He also authored a bundle of books that many subsequent Dauphin County historians have treated as sacred texts.

It should be acknowledged that Egle, like most historians of the period, mixed ample folklore with fact. No one expected that a nineteenth-century historian could prove everything he wrote, although Egle often did quote from historical documents. "His writing, like everyone's at that time, was one-half scholarship, one-half what he knew to be true," explains Warren Wirebach, librarian at the Dauphin County Historical Society. For example, Wirebach says, Egle knew John Harris Jr.'s grandchildren and accepted stories from them as fact.

It also should be noted that Egle's writing period—from the 1870s through the 1890s—coincided with the end of the Indian wars in the West. Many Americans had little sympathy for the holdout tribes in Arizona, Montana and the Dakotas. Egle's commentary on the last natives of Lancaster County, who had been eliminated more than a century earlier, may reflect a late nineteenth-century bias against the last combative Indians in America.

But when it came to defending the Paxton Rangers, Egle went beyond folklore and even bias. More than most historians, he accepted almost all of Conyngham's work, reprinting much of the 1843 newspaper series in his own books. Then he created additional anti-Indian documents.

Egle wrote frequently about the massacre and the march on Philadelphia. In *An Illustrated History of the Commonwealth of Pennsylvania*; *History of Dauphin County*; *Notes and Queries* and other works, Egle was one of the first historians to make a case for the Paxton Boys as revolutionaries before the Revolution. He idealized them as pioneers of democracy who bravely challenged Philadelphia to provide for frontier justice and equal political representation.

In Egle's view, pre-Conyngham historians had misrepresented the Paxton Boys. Revision was necessary, he wrote in *Notes and Queries* (1895), "for the purpose of throwing aside the veil of obloquy which fanatical fury for over a century has covered the gallant frontiersmen of Paxtang, who loved their homes and their darling ones too well to tolerate a nest of copper-colored vipers in their midst."

For his account of the massacre, Egle relied heavily on Conyngham's bogus history, especially the Smith and Stewart letters. He then extended the deception by creating two new affidavits that Lancaster County's magistrates allegedly took against the Conestogas in the winter of 1764. In his *History of Dauphin County*, Egle reprinted the entire *Apology of the Paxton Volunteers*, including the affidavits that break the text. But instead of the six affidavits published in the original, Egle published eight.[22]

Forty years after Redmond Conyngham had created a new story line for the Rangers, Egle added to it by presenting affidavits supposedly collected by Paxton magistrate Thomas Forster from Matthew Cowden and Moses Dickey, Forster's Paxton neighbors. These additions increased to eleven the total number of individuals claimed as 1764 deponents by various writers.

In *An Illustrated History of the Commonwealth of Pennsylvania*, Egle echoed a spurious Conyngham claim: "It is well known that an investigation was had into the matter, by the magistrate (Shippen), at Lancaster, but the evidence against the Indians was so condemnatory that it was *not only suppressed but destroyed*." After so much anti-Indian evidence had been eliminated (a charge made only by Egle and Conyngham), Egle must have believed that a few more fabricated affidavits would do no harm.

Egle's Cowden testified, in tortured prose, that he had "remonstrated with old Seaheas harboring so many strange Indians who were suspected murdering ye back [frontier] inhabitants; when he replyed that he was to stand for them, meaning that he was not responsible, and the settlers must look out for themselves."

Egle's Dickey said that while scouting in the summer of 1763, he had seen Will Sock and two other Conestogas "on a march with strange Indians." The next day Dickey learned that several houses had been burned and families murdered in that area "and he fully believes Bill Soc and his companions done it."

Even if these affidavits were authentic—even though they surfaced, without explanation, 120 years after the massacre—their hearsay charges against the Conestogas would be compromised by their reputed authors' familial connections. Cowden, born Scots-Irish in Northern Ireland, had served as a captain of the Paxton Rangers and was a member of Paxton

Presbyterian. His grandson married John Elder's granddaughter. Dickey, also an Irish-born Scots-Irishman, lived right next to his church, Paxton Presbyterian, and is buried in its graveyard. His daughter married Thomas Forster's brother. His widow married Matthew Smith.

Egle, of Swiss-German heritage, maintained that he was not biased toward a Scots-Irish Presbyterian reading of history, but that claim is difficult to accept given his determination to cloister the Paxton Rangers from all guilt. In *An Illustrated History*, Egle wrote: "In the light of history, through recent research, it is time that [the Rangers'] conduct be justified, and the wrong done them righted."

As a historian and genealogist intimately familiar with biographies of the influential families of the Harrisburg area, Egle must have decided that a provincial need to justify the Rangers' conduct legitimized "recent research" that invented documents.

CHAPTER 9

"The Innocent Were Destined to Share the Fate of the Guilty"

In the three decades following publication of Redmond Conyngham's creative newspaper history of the Conestoga massacre, several local authors used his phony documents to help fashion their own accounts. So the story line changed, although not so much as Conyngham might have wished. As had earlier historians, most of these writers condemned the massacre. But post-Conyngham historians spent more time describing, if not justifying, the motivations of the Paxton Rangers. They could do that because they had freshly minted materials to help them "balance" the story.

Just two years after the newspaper accounts appeared, I. Daniel Rupp concentrated on establishing the "treacherous" nature of the Conestogas as providers of information to hostile Indians in his *History of Lancaster and York Counties*. The author cited Conyngham directly only once, but the newspaper articles' influence is evident throughout his work.

Rupp also quoted five of the 1764 deponents against the Conestogas. He particularly liked Marie LeRoy, who had testified that Will Sock's mother thought he was good for nothing. As if that maternal remark was insufficient, Rupp added another mother's opinion in a footnote. He said one Jacob Bachman had claimed that his mother had met Sock— "but she never liked his countenance—guilt played upon it."

In his history of Dauphin and nearby counties the next year, Rupp provided a similar defense of the Rangers, with a special emphasis on the efforts of "their endeared pastor," John Elder, to save the Conestogas from the wrath of the Paxtonians. By the mid-1840s, Rupp made Conyngham's fabrications and the anti-Indian depositions essential parts of the massacre story in central Pennsylvania.

George H. Morgan termed the massacre "unjustifiable" in his *Annals of Harrisburg* (1858), the first history of the Harrisburg area to describe the incident. But he also said the Paxton Rangers had plenty of provocation from the Indians and no support from the government; therefore, they were "governed by usages of their own."

Morgan and two local historians who followed him all suffered from Conyngham's creations. They quoted from the bogus Matthew Smith letter (the Rangers killed the Indians in self-defense) and all defended Lazarus Stewart's role as a Ranger leader, a role that had not existed until Conyngham invented it. But the other historians—Jacob I. Mombert in *An Authentic History of Lancaster County in the State of Pennsylvania* (1869) and Alexander Harris in *A Biographical History of Lancaster County* (1872)—did more than simply quote Rangers who were, as Mombert explained it, "goaded to desperation by repeated murders perpetrated by Indians." They also criticized the killers and the community's leaders.

Mombert, who served as pastor of Lancaster's St. James Episcopal during the Civil War, said the Rangers' "lawless conduct cannot be justified any more than their indiscriminate slaughter of suspected murderers and helpless old men, women and innocent children." He also quoted Gordon's *History of Pennsylvania*: "It is not possible to exculpate the magistrates of the town."

Harris, in describing the depth of anti-Indian feeling in 1763, also incriminated the community's leadership: "Never was hatred more deep and general than on the Pennsylvania frontier at this period," he wrote. "It was by no means confined to the vulgar. Magistrates, and even the clergy shared it, and it is not surprising that it found a vent."

In the second half of the nineteenth century, two significant national historians described the massacre of the Conestogas in some depth. Their assessments could not have been more different, in part because one used Conyngham as a source and one did not.

In his influential two-volume study, *The Conspiracy of Pontiac* (1870), Francis Parkman devoted forty pages to the massacre in Lancaster and the march on Philadelphia. The author believed that the Conestogas, like the western Indians of his own era, deserved their fate because they were an inferior race, doomed to fall as civilization progressed. He emphasized historical materials that supported this bias.

Parkman said Indian atrocities had driven the Rangers to violence; blamed the murders on "the more violent class"; and absolved John

Elder, Lazarus Stewart and other individuals of guilt. "The exasperated frontiersmen were not in a mood to discriminate," he explained, "and the innocent were destined to share the fate of the guilty."

Conyngham had no more loyal adherent than Parkman. The Stewart, Smith and Donnally documents directed the historian's retelling of the story. Parkman actually proposed that Smith's bogus account must be accurate because Stewart's bogus account confirmed it. In a footnote, Parkman praised Conyngham: "This gentleman employed himself with most unwearied diligence in collecting a voluminous mass of documents, comprising, perhaps, every thing that could contribute to extenuate the conduct of the Paxton men." In an appendix, Parkman reprinted Conyngham's texts of six of the 1764 deponents, making questionable documents damaging to the Conestogas available for the first time to historians and a general audience outside central Pennsylvania.

By contrast, in *A Century of Dishonor* (1881), Helen Hunt Jackson ignored Conyngham and referred to earlier accounts composed by Rhoda Barber, William Henry Jr., Benjamin Franklin and Thomas Barton.

An active opponent of duplicitous government policies toward Indians in her time, Jackson did something else Parkman and most nineteenth-century historians never considered: she introduced the Conestogas as a significant tribe of people, with a long history and distinct culture, all of which ended abruptly in December 1763.

"It is impossible to read now these accounts of the massacres of defenseless and peaceable Indians in the middle of the eighteenth century, without the reflection that the record of the nineteenth is blackened by the same stains," the author noted in a chapter on several massacres. She described the Conestoga slaughter first. "What Pennsylvania pioneers did in 1763 to helpless and peaceable Indians of Conestoga," she concluded, "Colorado pioneers did in 1864 to helpless and peaceable Cheyennes at Sand Creek, and have threatened to do again to helpless and peaceable Utes in 1880."

At the time of publication, the impact of Jackson's book, unlike Parkman's, was minimal. Jackson's novel, *Ramona*, about the poor treatment of Indians in Southern California, was considerably more popular. Time has altered the response. *A Century of Dishonor* probably is more widely read than *The Conspiracy of Pontiac* today by general readers; but Parkman's take on the Conestoga massacre remains more familiar to historians.

Following Parkman and Jackson, seven decades would pass before anyone with a national audience would discuss the killing of the Conestogas in depth. Brooke Hindle's "The March of the Paxton Boys," the first modern scholarly study, appeared in the *William and Mary Quarterly* in 1946. Hindle discussed the Conestoga massacre before rushing to embrace the image of the Paxton Boys as early revolutionaries that Egle and Charles H. Lincoln (*The Revolutionary Movement in Pennsylvania*, 1901) had painted. Hindle seemed even more certain that "the march of the Paxton Boys paved the way for internal revolution."

A young University of Pennsylvania assistant history instructor at the time, Hindle relied heavily on Conyngham in defending the roles of Elder, Stewart and Smith. While he went on to become a renowned historian of science, Hindle's footnotes referencing Conyngham in this early article further corrupted the record of the Indian killings and introduced historians of frontier relations to false documents they otherwise might not have encountered.

John Raine Dunbar provided the next scholarly assessment, and one of the most extensive, in his introduction to *The Paxton Papers*, a 1957 compilation of nearly half of the sixty-odd pamphlets published following the massacre and march. Anyone who has seriously examined the Paxton Boys in the past half century has read this book.

Dunbar, who taught literature at Claremont McKenna College in California, tried to provide a fair appraisal of the Conestoga massacre. He quoted extensively from letters by Shippen, Penn and Elder but also relied on Conyngham's Smith and Stewart letters. He did not find the affidavits damning the Conestogas persuasive.

Dunbar revived questions that had been asked immediately following the massacre, although he made little effort to answer them:

> *Why did not Colonel Robinson* [sic] *and his Highlanders, who were in Lancaster, protect the Indians? What were the magistrates doing? Many statements were made about Colonel Robinson's part in the affair: he offered his assistance and the magistrates refused it; he did nothing; he replied "D-n them, I would not care if the whole race were slain, for my company has suffered enough by them already. I will not stir one step." There was a similar difference of opinion about the actions of the magistrates at Lancaster: they did all in their power to prevent it; they did nothing at all; they connived at the killing.*

Paul A.W. Wallace (*Indians in Pennsylvania*, 1961) was one of the first writers to describe the Paxton Boys as "Indian haters." In a brief account of the massacre, the historian provided no extenuating explanations for the militiamen's conduct, writing: "By the Conestoga massacres the Paxton Boys drew attention to a new intolerance in Pennsylvania and also to a growing division between the frontier and the older settled country."[23]

Hubertis M. Cummings, a research historian with the Pennsylvania Historical and Museum Commission in the early decades of the century, described the Conestoga massacre in depth, but from a compromised perspective. As a Scots-Irish graduate of Princeton, a Harrisburg-area resident and a member of Paxton Presbyterian Church, Cummings occasionally allowed his loyalty to those who had dispensed what he termed "rude frontier justice" to overcome his objectivity.

Cummings relied largely on Parkman and Egle. He repeated Conyngham/Smith's portrayal of the attack on Indian Town but not the workhouse. His *Scots Breed and Susquehanna*, published posthumously in 1964, explained that the Paxton Rangers had traced "marauding Indians" to Conestoga "and none found it difficult to believe that those who harbored the foe also were the foe."

Cummings noted that historians would remain divided on how to view the massacre. "Which was worse," he asked, "the inaction of a body of lawmakers, or the direct brute action of a body of men whose children and families had been left unprotected by Government?"

However other historians answered that question, Cummings was determined that John Elder, first pastor of Cummings's church, should not be tainted in any way. The author took pains in *Scots Breed* and even more so in another posthumous publication to promote "the Fighting Parson." Cummings said in a 1966 *Journal of Presbyterian History* article, "He could neither encourage riot nor condone massacre. He sincerely wished to be true to himself as a man and as an ordained servant of God."

Also in that article, Cummings was first to point out a flaw in Conyngham's account. Nothing in Elder's or anyone else's correspondence in the eighteenth century suggested that Elder on horseback personally tried to stop the Rangers, Cummings said. That Conyngham tale, he advised, "had best be regarded as mere legend, whatever its excellence as narrative."

In 1967, Wilbur R. Jacobs provided balanced, document-guided instruction on *The Paxton Riots and the Frontier Theory* as part of *The Berkeley Series in American History*. The University of California–Santa Barbara professor touched only lightly on the massacre (as described by Conyngham/Smith and others) before detailing the grievances the Paxton Boys presented in Philadelphia. Jacobs favored the Egle-Hindle theory that the Paxton Boys struck an early blow for democracy. He only seemed to offer another option by asking this loaded question near the end of his text: "Were the Paxton Boys more interested in killing Indians or in extending democracy?"[24]

Frank J. Cavaioli, a history professor with the State University of New York, contributed a controversial article, "Profile of the Paxton Boys: Murderers of the Conestoga Indians," to the Lancaster County Historical Society's *Journal* in 1983. The article named five Paxton Boys, although the only serious "proof" the author provided for any of them actually riding with the Rangers to kill the Conestogas came directly from the Conyngham narratives of Smith and Stewart.

It is instructive that 140 years after Redmond Conyngham created his massacre documents the texts appeared verbatim in a scholarly paper. To historians who did not verify sources, the invented documents of 1843 had become as real as authentic materials.

George Franz might have changed that with his exposé of Conyngham's documents in 1989. But *Paxton: A Study of Community Structure and Mobility in the Colonial Pennsylvania Backcountry* was primarily devoted to describing the early community and individuals of Paxton Township. The author spent little time detailing the Rangers' activities in Lancaster and Philadelphia. He relegated his complaint against Conyngham to an appendix, which has barely been acknowledged in the scholarly community.

CHAPTER 10

"A Zone of Vicious Racial Violence"

Some historians at the turn of the twenty-first century continued to see the American Indian as little more than a temporary foil of Manifest Destiny. But others turned 180 degrees to assess the impact of European immigrants on the native population.

Revisionist historians, Daniel Richter and James Merrell among them, promoted study of the original inhabitants as a way to provide "a new, inclusive way of getting to the heart of the early American experience." Others had more radical views. Francis Jennings said that he believed the traditional "discovery" of the New World more appropriately should be characterized as an "invasion."

While reevaluating Indian–European relations on the colonial frontier—the "backcountry," as many historians term it—writers influenced by the Red Power and civil rights movements focused on racial animosity. They tended to view the French and Indian War, Pontiac's Rebellion and, especially, the massacre of the Conestogas in red and white.

"Frontier frustrations and racial antagonism reached a symbolic climax in December 1763 when a band of Lancaster County ruffians slaughtered twenty friendly Indians," wrote Alden T. Vaughan in an influential 1984 *Pennsylvania History* essay, "Frontier Banditti and the Indians: The Paxton Boys' Legacy, 1763–1775."

Vaughan, a Columbia University historian of race relations, believed that racism motivated the Paxton Boys and their supporters. He said an anti–Paxton Boys pamphleteer in 1764 only slightly exaggerated the frontier position when he had a fictional spokesman declare of Indians, "If I tho't that any of their Colour was to be admitted into the Heavenly World, I would not desire to go there myself." Vaughan further believed that the inability of Pennsylvania's government to apprehend and punish the Conestogas' killers set loose a "lawless Banditti" to prey on Indians after 1763. The result was more than political and denominational strife among white men, he wrote: "The Paxton Boys' principal legacy was 'open season' on the Indians, friend or foe, a circumstance the Indians surely remembered when they chose sides in the American Revolution."

The irrepressibly pro-Indian historian Francis Jennings in *Empire of Fortune* (1988) cited the Conestoga massacre as "at least one example of a lynching" in Pennsylvania during the French and Indian War. Although he did not cite race specifically as a motivating factor in the Conestoga massacre, his repeated use of the word "lynching" implies as much.[25] Moreover, Jennings, a former director of the Newberry Library's Indian history center, asserted that the killings at the workhouse followed "a proclamation for the arrest and punishment of the lynchers, which was ignored although their identity was no secret. The magistrates of Lancaster collected the remaining Conestogas into the public workhouse in order to protect them. Their act merely made the next slaughter easier by bringing all of its intended victims together."

Thomas P. Slaughter also charged the Paxton Boys as racists in a January 1991 article on eighteenth-century violence published in the *Pennsylvania Magazine of History and Biography*. Slaughter, who now teaches history at the University of Rochester, maintained that the Paxtonians were particularly outraged because the Conestogas had been Christianized and wore European clothes, thereby threatening men insecure about their identity as members of the dominant culture at the edge of the frontier. He described white settlers as "conscious of being in between their native culture and those, generally Indians, against whom they defined themselves. Thus, the whites acted out, in horrible fashion, their own cultural liminality and that of their victims."

James Merrell, who focused on treaties and their negotiators in his groundbreaking 1999 work, *Into the American Woods: Negotiators on the Pennsylvania Frontier*, sympathetically presented the positions of both Conestogas and Paxtonians.

The Vassar College historian retold the massacre story with spare details. He employed the account of the carnage in the workhouse yard by William Henry Jr., which he credited to John Heckewelder, and an account of the storming of the workhouse, which he credited to no one. In fact, the numbers in Merrell's description of the attack on the workhouse—twelve Rangers stayed outside, three broke down the door, five covered the "jailers" and the rest went for the Indians—came from Redmond Conyngham's irrepressible Matthew Smith letter.

Rather than decry the murder of the Conestogas, Merrell lamented the death of the negotiating process. By killing Indians in Lancaster and threatening to kill more in Philadelphia, Merrell said, the Rangers ruined long-standing peace efforts that could be traced to a treasured document of the Conestogas: the treaty with William Penn of 1701. Many subsequent treaty sessions had been held, Merrell wrote, but "now both Conestoga and Lancaster had seen meetings of a different sort. Now they sat, bloody ground, mute repudiation of council culture and all that it stood for."

In 2001, Daniel Richter, director of the McNeil Center for Early American Studies at the University of Pennsylvania, published a widely read and critically acclaimed book presenting colonial history from the Indian perspective. *Facing East from Indian Country: A Native History of Early America* profoundly altered the established story line.

Richter argued that conflict between inhabitants and invaders had become racial by the mid-eighteenth century. While Pontiac's forces singled out white settlers and spared blacks, he wrote, the Paxton Boys "nursed their own vision of racial exclusivity on a continent purged of their enemies."

The primary enemy at Indian Town was Will Sock, Richter noted, because Paxtonians believed he had "not only duplicitously consorted with enemy Indians but had himself killed and captured Pennsylvanians." Richter believed, however, that Sock "may have been guilty of nothing more than holding his head high, speaking disrespectfully to his Euro-American neighbors, and maintaining communications with kin who lived in Indian country."

Richter credited Merrell with providing the information on which he based his brief description of the massacre. By embracing part of Matthew Smith's account through Merrell, therefore, Richter also reflected Conyngham's curse.

But the author concluded with a much larger view:

> *The crusades of 1763 crystallized long-simmering hatred into explicit new doctrines of racial unity and racial antagonism. In parallel ways, Pontiac and the Paxton Boys preached the novel idea that all Native people were "Indians," that all Euro-Americans were "Whites," and that all on one side must unite to destroy the other. Thus the formerly parallel worlds of eighteenth-century North America crashed together.*

Taking a different approach, Gregory Dowd, director of Native American Studies at the University of Michigan, argued that the Paxton Boys not only killed the Conestogas but also won almost every point in their dispute over the status of Indians. "Nobody faced charges for the Conestoga murders," he wrote in *War under Heaven: Pontiac, The Indian Nations, and the British Empire* (2002). "Before those killings, the government had been reluctant to reimburse locally organized bands that went out to patrol the frontiers; in the same month as the Paxtonians' march [on Philadelphia], the Assembly agreed to reimburse two such bands. By the end of the winter, the government had embraced the policy of Indian removal and was struggling to carry it out."

Dowd also commented on specific points related to the massacre. The Royal Scottish Highlanders may have had good reason not to intervene to protect the Conestogas, he observed, "but their inaction cast doubt on the willingness of the king's troops to protect Indians from British subjects." And, speculatively, he tied John Elder's discharge from command of the Rangers directly to his refusal to name any Ranger who participated in the massacre.

After providing a bare-bones description of the massacre entirely sympathetic to the Conestogas, Jane Merritt analyzed the Paxton Boys in *At the Crossroads: Indians & Empires on a Mid-Atlantic Frontier, 1700–1763* (2003). The Old Dominion University professor emphasized racial hatred. She argued that the Paxton Rangers annihilated the peaceful Conestogas not only because they blamed all Indians for the hostile acts of some but also because killing government-protected Indians was a way of retaliating against political leaders who ignored frontiersmen or, worse, considered them "Christian white savages."

The Conestoga massacre played a central role in a 2004 collection of essays entitled *Friends & Enemies in Penn's Woods: Indians, Colonists, and the Racial Construction of Pennsylvania.* Editors William Pencak, a historian at Penn State University, and Daniel Richter set out to explain how the harmonious relationship that followed William Penn's original treaty with Indians in 1682 could have disintegrated into the Conestoga slaughter of 1763. The editors adopted racial animosity as their theme, writing in the introduction: "The frontiers of Pennsylvania may have been the first place on the continent where 'Reds' and 'Whites' consciously battled each other as racially defined groups."

One of the book's essays provided a fresh take on the Paxton Boys' motivations. Krista Camenzind, in a distillation of a dissertation completed at the University of California–San Diego, accepted the Paxton Boys' uprising as an act of racial violence. But, she added, "The creation of a racial enemy entailed an evolution in thinking, and it served a specific, gendered purpose for frontier Pennsylvanians. By creating a racial enemy, Euro-American frontiersmen were able to legitimate an act of cowardice—killing unarmed men, women, and children—as an act of male valor."

Colin Calloway's *The Scratch of a Pen: 1763 and the Transformation of North America* (2006) reconsidered Indian–European relations during a crucial period. By concentrating on the year of the Treaty of Paris and other transformational events, Calloway, a professor of history and Native American studies at Dartmouth College, ensured that the Conestoga massacre would play a significant role in his work.

Calloway provided an outline of the massacre in a manner entirely sympathetic to the Conestogas. Following the massacre, he wrote, any common ground was "shrinking fast in an atmosphere of escalating race hatred. If the Conestogas' Christianity could not save them from the wrath of Christians, what basis could there be for coexistence?" By 1763, Calloway concluded, echoing Pencak and Richter, William Penn's peaceable kingdom had become "a zone of vicious racial violence."

Princeton University historian Peter Silver asserted in *Our Savage Neighbors: How Indian War Transformed Early America* (2007) that the Conestogas were "conspicuously, heartbreakingly nonbelligerent." They were murdered, he said, in "a stereotyped, detail-by-detail reenactment of how Indian attacks on rural farmhouses had unfolded during the war." Silver characterized the Conestoga killings not as crimes of passion but as a way to intimidate other Indians and redirect government protection from peace-professing Indians to frontier settlers.

Kevin Kenny's *Peaceable Kingdom Lost: The Paxton Boys and the Destruction of William Penn's Holy Experiment* (2009) followed Daniel Richter and others in providing a solid case for the massacre of the Conestogas as the central event that poisoned Indian–white relations in colonial Pennsylvania. "The Paxton Boys made no distinction between 'friendly' and 'enemy' Indians in 1763," the Boston College history professor observed. "They chose to kill the Conestogas precisely because they were peaceful and lived under government protection." He suggested that local officials paved the way for the attacks, and he maintained that afterward, other outlaws believed the killing season for Indians was always open.

Kenny repeatedly blasted Governor John Penn for doing nothing to apprehend the Paxton Boys and correctly identified Edward Shippen as "the proprietary official most directly accountable in this affair." But the author's comments about the supposed murderers are, curiously, contradictory.

While he claimed Lazarus Stewart's massacre account is "unverified" and Matthew Smith's "fabricated," Kenny nevertheless said he believed the two men participated in the killings because they were "identified in most accounts as the leaders of the Lancaster massacre."

Most accounts, of course, including Kenny's, have been influenced by Redmond Conyngham.

Aside from these and other academic historians who have written in recent years about the massacre within larger works, two Native Americans have written short books about the killings from a radically Indian-centered point of view. Hyhotah, also known as Terry Lee Silverchain, and Jessie Marafioti both claim their ancestors survived the slaughter.

Hyhotah, a Mohawk living in North Carolina, comes from a storytelling tradition: he relies more on legend than fact. *Gonacagoa* (1999) is marred by silly historical inaccuracies and murky mysticism. But it also contains some disturbing images of the massacres at Indian Town and in Lancaster that are not easy to ignore.

Violent Indian haters called "paxtons" killed the Conestogas, Hyhotah wrote. He maintained that ministers led the rabble, and he said the primary minister at both massacre sites wore a black robe and a silver belt buckle engraved with an Anglican cross. Hyhotah quoted a Lancaster resident describing the scene as the Paxton Rangers left the second massacre: "They were holding scalps in the air while the black robe was cursing, holding his bible to the sky quoting the scriptures that say, 'I will give you the heathen savage for your sake…' Many of our people know that the judge in Lancaster was behind the massacre and now we have great fear of being targeted for much the same treatment from the law of this town."

By accusing a minister and a magistrate as instigators, Hyhotah echoed early historians who wondered whether Lancaster County's leaders had helped set up the killings.

Blessed Are the Peacemakers: A Survivor's Tale from the Massacre at Conestoga Manor (2005) makes an assertion found nowhere else in massacre literature. Marafioti, a part-Indian resident of Dalhart, Texas, said her grandmother told her the first killings took place in a church near Indian Town. The six Conestogas were worshipping along with an unidentified number of Lenapes when the Paxton Rangers struck.

The author said she understood that her grandmother's version of what happened differed from other accounts. "The massacre of 1763 was recorded by white men," she explained. "Those men failed to mention the people were in church." She implied that the omission of the church was part of an effort to deny that the Indians were a religious and peaceful people. Marafioti said the Indians were reciting the Lord's Prayer as their murderers shouted, "You lying heathens," "You no good redskins, how dare you farm alongside us good white folks?" "The only good Indian is a dead one," and "What makes you think Jesus wants to hear your prayers?"

The massacre did not occur in a church. Marafioti's account is as ahistorical as Hyhotah's, and both are designed to present the Indians' murderers in the worst possible light. In that respect, these stories are mirror images of nineteenth-century efforts to enhance the reputation of the Paxton Boys by distorting the facts.

But the Indian writers claimed to understand something deeper than the documented facts of what happened in December 1763. They claimed that the militia, ministers and magistrates committed a crime so perverse that official records could not contain it.

PART 3

Killers and Abettors

CHAPTER 11
"The Most Respectable of Men"

In a formal message to Governor John Penn in January 1768—more than four years after the Conestoga massacre—the Pennsylvania Assembly charged that the Indian killers still could be identified, "for when we consider the Manner of committing the Murders at Lancaster; that it was done at Noon-Day, in the midst of a Populous Borough, and in the Presence of many spectators by Men probably of the same County, undisguised and well known, we apprehend their Names may be easily discovered."

But their names were not easily discovered. In the nearly 250 years since the men from Paxton slaughtered twenty unarmed Conestogas, most of them during a very public display of wrath followed by jubilant horseplay, many historians have commented on the activities of the Paxton Rangers as a group, but no one has determined with certainty the name of any individual murderer. All of the victims have names. None of the killers is known.

Recoiling from the hostilities of the French and Indian War and Pontiac's uprising, many residents of Lancaster County approved of or were indifferent to the massacre of the Conestogas. They had no reason to name the killers.

The Rangers apparently intimidated everyone else into remaining silent. The Quaker James Wright, one of Lancaster County's delegates to the Pennsylvania Assembly and a government-appointed caretaker for the Conestogas, might have been expected to identify the Rangers he knew. In fact, John Fanning Watson's *Annals of Philadelphia and Pennsylvania* reported in 1857 that Wright "well remembered" the killers and had told a fellow legislator that he had "survived nearly the whole of them, and that they generally came to untimely or suffering deaths!"

But even though he may have been pleased that the murderers died—suffering—before he did, Wright never named them in public. Susanna Wright may have explained her brother's reluctance to identify individual Rangers in a January 16, 1764 letter to the Quaker merchant Isaac Whitlock, in Lancaster. She told him that Paxton vigilantes were roaming throughout the region, making threats not only against other Indians but also against Israel Pemberton, leader of the assembly's Quakers, as well as against her brother.

Early historians speculated about who might have killed the Indians. No one offered proof. Only one contemporary historian has made a sustained effort to identify the Paxton raiders. He failed.

George Franz originally had planned to write a book about the individuals involved in the massacre and the march on Philadelphia. He borrowed the idea from Richard Maxwell Brown's book that identified the South Carolina Regulators through tax records and other sources. But Franz could not identify, with certainty, any of the individuals. So in 1989 he published, instead, his book about the Paxton community: *Paxton, a Study of Community Structure and Mobility*.

"I tried for five years and got what I could, but I couldn't track down the individuals," Franz explains now. "It was hard to know who they were, in part because they kept their identities secret. My guess is most were members of the Paxton Presbyterian Church and Donegal Presbyterian Church. It is clear that the Presbyterian Church was organizing this group, ostensibly to protect the frontier."

The part played by Presbyterians is exceptionally clear. Many of the buds that bloomed into the Conestoga massacre were transplanted from the pulpit to the pews of Paxton Presbyterian Church.[26]

Scots-Irish pioneers piled up rough limestone rocks to form Paxton Presbyterian in 1740. They hauled the rocks from surrounding farms and, according to one source, lubricated their efforts with ample portions of whiskey. Their enduring stone church stands on high ground about three miles east of the Susquehanna River in Harrisburg's eastern suburbs. It is the oldest Presbyterian church in continuous use in Pennsylvania.

Paxton Presbyterian is proud of its long history and stores mementos of it in display cases in a vestibule connecting the original sanctuary with an extensive church addition. The most curious item is a patriotic ribbon inscribed: "Law and Order—The Paxton Boys." Church historian Ron Wix, a longtime member of the congregation, doesn't know the origin of

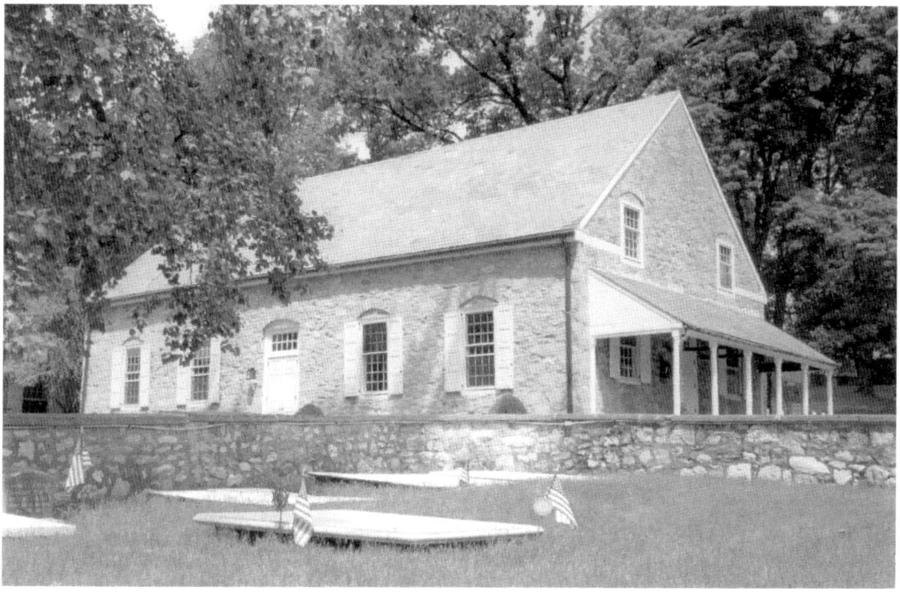

Paxton Presbyterian Church, constructed in 1740, with gravestone of church minister and Paxton Ranger commander John Elder in the foreground. *Photo by the author.*

this artifact, but he knows why an item associated with the Paxton Boys is kept here: the "Boys" are forever linked not only with vigilantism but also with this church.

John Elder, commander of the Paxton Rangers, served as the congregation's second and practically lifelong pastor. Two of his sons, Robert and Joshua, were Rangers and are buried near their father in the stone-walled cemetery adjacent to the church. A number of Elder's parishioners were Rangers. Cowdens and Kelsos, Ritcheys and Rutherfords, some of whom no doubt served as Rangers, lie nearby.

Rangers and church members certainly formed the nucleus of the Conestoga raiders. Elder would not have tried to stop them—or claimed to have tried—if many of the riders had not been his militiamen and parishioners. Unfortunately, church records don't help resolve which Paxton Presbyterian members might have ridden with the Rangers; those records burned in 1892.

Paxton Presbyterian's bicentennial history dances by the massacre without condemning anyone: "There were those who said [the Paxton Boys'] raids were justified…and there were those who saw no justification." Wix is equally nonjudgmental about the Paxton Boys—"They were either famous or infamous, depending on your point of view"—but not about the effect of the massacre on other Indians—"It got their attention."

No present church member claims descent from a Paxton Boy. Restless Scots-Irish, Wix explains, tended to keep moving west and left the congregation long ago. But, in fact, no one anywhere has claimed descent from someone who killed the Conestogas because the killers were not publicly identified during their lives and subsequent identifications are questionable or fraudulent.

But names have been named.

John Elder, like other Presbyterian ministers, exercised near-total authority as both spiritual and military leader of his community. No military action was initiated in northern Lancaster County without his knowledge and, probably, approval. Any investigation of the Paxton Rangers must begin with Elder.

Born, educated and licensed to preach in Scotland, Elder visited Ireland only briefly before immigrating to the United States and settling in Lancaster County. The Presbytery of Donegal ordained Elder in 1738, when he was thirty-two, and he was called to serve as pastor at Paxton and, subsequently and simultaneously, at neighboring Derry Presbyterian in present-day Hershey. Virtually until he died in 1792, Elder ministered to both congregations.

Elder owned a fair-sized farm about a mile from Paxton Presbyterian. His property was adjacent to the property of magistrate Thomas Forster and an easy walk away from the riverside home of John Harris Jr. Both were parishioners and close friends. Elder built his expansive house in 1740, the same year as his church, and he used similar coarse fieldstone. In that house, Elder's two successive wives, both named Mary, bore him fifteen children.[27]

When the French and Indian War began in 1754, Elder helped organize and arm members of the community. After the enemy attacked Paxton, he urged his parishioners to carry firearms to church and he preached to stir their wrath against the "invaders." According to legend, Elder brought his own musket and spoke with Bible in one hand, gun in the other. Many area historians, as well as Paxton Presbyterian Church's website, have delighted in describing Elder as "the fighting parson." In this vein, William Henry Egle claimed that Indians believed musket balls that barely missed the minister had been "turned aside by the Good Spirit."

Elder may have had other close encounters with Indians. Lancaster historian I. Daniel Rupp said the minister "frequently" visited Indians at Conestoga and other places to chastise them for "admitting *stranger Indians* among them; conduct which made them suspected of treachery."[28]

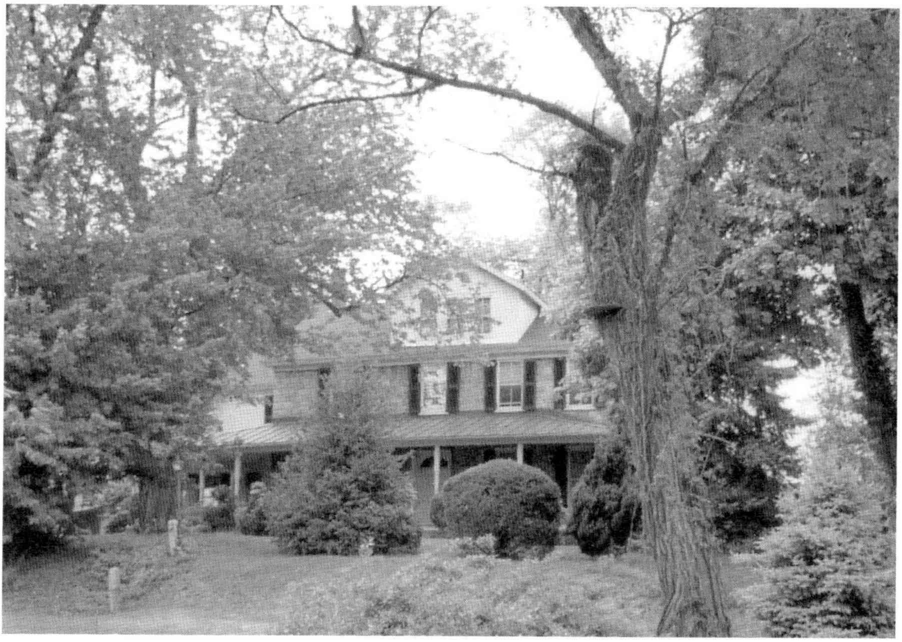

John Elder's house, constructed in 1740, is the oldest building still standing within the city of Harrisburg. *Photo by the author.*

With the advent of Pontiac's Rebellion, Elder's role increased. Recognizing that local governments were weak, provincial authorities turned to ministers for leadership. In July 1763, Governor James Hamilton authorized Elder to raise two companies of fifty men each "for the defense of the Frontier against the incursion of the Indians." Hamilton authorized these units particularly "to cover & protect, during the Harvest, such of the Inhabitants as by their remote situation are most exposed to the incursions of the Enemy."[29]

Each company would have a captain, lieutenant and ensign; two sergeants; two corporals; and forty-three privates. Hamilton appointed only one of these men: Asher Clayton, the man who eventually would replace Elder, would serve as captain of one of the companies. Elder chose the other captain, Timothy Green, a member of his congregation at Paxton Presbyterian. Lieutenant John Likens and Ensign James Forster served in Clayton's company. Lieutenant Jacob Ludwig and Ensign Charles Stewart joined Green.

But no one has ever associated any of these officers with the attacks on Conestoga and Lancaster, and the rosters of enlisted men in Elder's two companies, like a lot of things associated with the Rangers, have not survived.

Elder made it clear in a series of letters to the governor that he initially had a hard time finding and retaining soldiers who would rather have stayed home to defend their families while tending their crops. John Harris Jr. collaborated with Elder, helping to find the necessary arms, food and other supplies to keep the two companies in the field. The Rangers' ranks filled as the companies made their adventurous excursions upriver in August and October.

Then came the easy slaughter at Conestoga and Lancaster. Elder discussed the massacre in only two extant letters: the December 16, 1763 letter to the governor and the February 1, 1764 letter to Edward Shippen's son, Joseph.

In the earlier letter, in which he called the killers "hot headed ill advised persons," Elder said that he had received information on December 13 that "a number of persons were assembling on purpose to go to cut off the Indians at Conestogo." He claimed that he and Magistrate Forster had sent a written message asking these men to desist. He said he had informed the vigilantes that they might be sentenced to death if they killed Indians under government protection. And he said he had told them they should not expect the populace to shield their identities.

So the minister admitted that he knew about the plot to kill the Conestogas a day in advance. But if he provided a warning—and there is no record that he did—it was ignored.

In the February 1 letter, Elder said the Paxton Boys' impending march on Philadelphia could not be stopped, and the marchers "have the good wishes of the country in general." He said he had "always used my utmost endeavours to discourage these proceedings," but he had failed because the Paxton Boys were so "exasperated" by the Quakers' protection of Indians. Elder also defended Presbyterians and the Scots-Irish and said they should not be blamed as groups for killing the Conestogas.

Three times in this letter Elder said no one could stop the Paxton Boys. "It's in vain, nay even unsafe for any one to oppose their measures," he said. And he said Edward Shippen ("tho' a gentlem'n highly esteemed by the frontier inhabitants") would find it "useless if not dangerous" to stand in opposition. Finally, in a defense of Harris, who was "gravely misrepresented in Philad'a…as the chief promoter of these riots," Elder reported that his neighbor "has acted as much in opposition to these measures as he could with any safety in his situation."

In sum, Elder maintained that anyone who could have exerted influence over the assaults on Lancaster and Philadelphia had decided it would be futile and perilous to oppose them.

But Peter Seibert, a Harrisburg native and historian who has studied Elder's life and lectured on his role in the Paxton community for many years, believes the minister/commander controlled the situation from the beginning. "For Elder to play the role of the patsy, the role of the man who couldn't stop the Paxton Boys, just doesn't fit," he comments. "Elder was in charge. I think he instigated the massacre."

Early historians had no doubt about Elder's influence. The earliest, Robert Proud, maintained that "the perpetrators of this deed were led on by a Presbyterian minister, persuading themselves that they were doing God's work by extirpating the heathen from the earth."

But it appears that Elder led from the pulpit, not from the saddle. There is no indication that he ever rode with armed Rangers up the branches of the Susquehanna, to Conestoga and Lancaster, or to Philadelphia. He was fifty-seven years old in 1763, decades older than rank-and-file Rangers and hardly fit to go riding around the countryside with them. Old men have always known how to persuade young men to fight for them. Recruiting, feeding and ministering to the Rangers kept Elder sufficiently occupied. As the primary rabble-rouser, he had blood in his heart, not on his hands.

The only individuals reported by name as traveling with the Paxton Boys to Philadelphia are Matthew Smith and James Gibson, who presented the frontiersmen's grievances; and Colonel John Armstrong, who added prestige to the expedition. A fourth man, William Brown, apparently accompanied them, but his name has a line drawn through it on a handwritten copy of the Paxtonian "Remonstrance" in the collections of the Lancaster County Historical Society.

Smith and Gibson are relatively shadowy men. Smith lived in Paxton; Gibson apparently lived elsewhere in Lancaster County. Both later fought in the Revolution. Smith served as vice-president of Pennsylvania for twelve days in 1779.

Armstrong was a man of considerable substance. Born in Ireland in 1717, he immigrated to Cumberland County as a young man and became a surveyor and community leader. At the outset of the French and Indian War, he took command of the militia west of the Susquehanna. He made his reputation by winning the battle of Kittanning and burning the town in 1756. Following the war, he returned to Carlisle and became a judge. Armstrong served as a major general in the opening battles of the Revolution. He was a member of the Continental Congress.

Brown, also identified as a Paxton Boy by H.M. Muhlenberg in the journal entries he kept during the Paxton uprising, is a total unknown.

There is no proof that any of these men had joined the earlier attacks on the Conestogas. In fact, Armstrong had a solid alibi: he was in Carlisle at the time.

The two writers known to have fashioned fraudulent documents to improve the reputation of the Scots-Irish provided the names of six men who supposedly rode with the Indian killers. Redmond Conyngham created from whole cloth leading roles in the massacre for Matthew Smith and Lazarus Stewart. William Henry Egle named four other men who might have participated.

Conyngham's chief antagonist, Lazarus Stewart, often is portrayed as the most violent Paxton Boy. This characterization is based only partially on his fabricated role as a leader of the attack on the Lancaster workhouse. Stewart may, indeed, have participated in the massacre, but he pursued a sufficiently violent documented military career without adding the scalps of the Conestogas to his belt.

He was born in Hanover Township in 1734. Later he lived in Paxton and attended Paxton Presbyterian Church. In 1755, when he was twenty-one years old, he rode with a company of volunteers in Braddock's expedition. Then he helped to guard settlements along the Juniata River. Stewart was a Paxton Ranger during Pontiac's Rebellion, but little is known about his service. In the autumn of 1763, he apparently was among the Rangers who found the Connecticut settlers who had been killed and mangled by Indians along the Susquehanna's North Branch.

In 1769, Stewart and others, calling themselves Paxton Boys, aligned themselves with surviving Connecticut settlers who laid claim to and were battling Pennsylvanians for control of the Wyoming Valley. Pennsylvania outlawed these defectors and, over the next several years, issued warrants against Stewart for murder, assault, riot, treason and arson. Stewart escaped three attempted arrests; he killed a man on the third attempt in 1772.

During this time, a minor official in Lebanon Township, Lancaster County, made the only known eighteenth-century allegation that Lazarus Stewart may have been one of the Conestogas' killers. Constable J.P. De Haas tried to arrest Stewart for the crime of arson in September 1770. De Haas said in a deposition that Stewart rebuffed him, clubbed him and followed him home. He would have followed him inside, but a family member locked the door behind De Haas. Stewart stood threateningly at the door for some time. According to De Haas, Stewart claimed that "there was long ago two hundred Pounds Reward offered for him." De Haas said he understood that this reward referred to "Stewart's being one of the Persons concerned in

Murdering the Indians in Lancaster Goal."[30] Then, De Haas said, Stewart "Rode off in Triumph."

The Pennsylvania Assembly rapidly embraced this constabular supposition, observing in a message to Governor Penn that "there is Cause to suspect the said Stewart hath been guilty of a Crime of a more atrocious Nature," and calling for Penn to offer a reward for apprehending Stewart. But Penn offered a fifty-pound reward for Stewart's apprehension only "for the Crime for which he was arrested." He did not mention the Conestoga massacre.

Given Penn's lack of interest in discovering the Indians' murderers in 1764, there is good reason to believe the governor would have had even less concern about charging anyone with that crime in 1770. Viewed another way, Penn reasonably might have thought that a constable's unsupported speculation was insufficient reason to charge a man with murder nearly seven years after a crime.

In any case, the commonwealth tolerated Lazarus Stewart for the better part of the next decade. Eventually, the Paxton Boys and the Connecticut settlers united with Pennsylvania settlers against the British during the Revolution. British soldiers shot and killed Stewart as he led a company of soldiers into the Battle of Wyoming, which the British won in the summer of 1778. He was forty-four years old.

The four men Egle named at various places in his prodigious output of overlapping and repetitive Pennsylvania and Dauphin County histories were William Boyd, Thomas Bell, John Reed and Frederick Parthemore. His brief notes about these men are based largely on hearsay.

Egle was most sure about Boyd. In *Pennsylvania Genealogies*, he said Boyd, born in Derry Township about 1733, "belonged to the Paxtang Boys, whose zeal in defense of their firesides compelled them to destroy the murdering savages of Conestoga." Boyd served as an officer during the French and Indian War and Revolution, but nowhere is he identified as an officer of the Paxton Rangers.

Egle said that a Kentuckian, John Graham, named Thomas Bell as a Paxton Ranger in a letter dated 1867. Bell, an elder in the Hanover Presbyterian Church later in life, was Graham's great-uncle. Graham supposedly told Egle, "My grandmother always said that Uncle Bell was one of the squad who were at Conestoga, but was not an elder in the church at the time."

Egle also reported that Blair Linn, author of *Buffalo Valley*, had said that Captain John Reed rode with the Rangers to Conestoga.

Egle published a letter from one Hiram Rutherford in *Notes and Queries* claiming that Frederick Parthemore was a Ranger. Egle did not directly dispute that possibility but said a story Rutherford told about Parthemore taking target practice before the raid on Conestoga actually occurred during the Revolution.

In addition to naming individual Rangers, but providing little or no information about them, Egle said Ranger descendants fondly remembered their ancestors as "the most respectable of men," an unsurprising vote of confidence from unidentified sources. Beyond that, Egle asserted that he personally had tracked the Rangers as a group through their lives. In *History of Dauphin County*, Egle said, "It is greatly to be lamented that all the names of those brave Paxtang boys have not been preserved to us, but those we have are sufficient to enable us to hurl back the imputation cast upon their memory."

Egle maintained that all of the "heroes of Conestoga" lived "long, valuable, and respected lives." In their later years, observed Egle, the Rangers included two elders in Old Hanover Presbyterian Church, "some of the most influential citizens of the Old Dominion," at least two signers of the Mecklenberg Declaration, several ministers and a college president. The descendant of another Paxton Boy, declared Egle with pride, became president of the United States. He did not name the president or anyone else.

Few other writers have bothered trying to identify individual Paxton Boys. Those who have are no more persuasive than Conyngham and Egle.

In a footnote to *The Conspiracy of Pontiac*, Francis Parkman retold a story from *Memoir of a Life Chiefly Passed in Pennsylvania* by Alexander Graydon. Supposedly a rifleman, identified only as "Davis," rode with the Paxton Boys to Philadelphia. Davis had claimed that another member of the group announced with pride that he was "the man who killed Will Sock—this is the arm that stabbed him to the heart, and I glory in it." But Davis did not name the man with the knife.

Henry W. Shoemaker, the Pennsylvania folklorist, mentioned another Paxton Ranger during a brief speech at the dedication of the Conestoga massacre memorial in Manor Township in 1924. Shoemaker said Simon Rostraver, a Presbyterian minister, in his youth had been a Ranger and had helped kill the Conestogas. Years after the massacre, according to Shoemaker, Rostraver was at the bedside of his dying granddaughter when he saw "an Indian whom he recognized as the Chief of the Conoys, whom he had personally massacred in Lancaster jail." The Indian soon disappeared and the girl died, events that the superstitious linked together, according to Shoemaker.

This story, which seems more romance than history, taps into a deep-rooted American tendency to view Indians as ghosts. Renee L. Bergland proposed in *The National Uncanny: Indian Ghosts and American Subjects* that Indians have haunted American life and literature since the seventeenth century. "When European Americans speak of Native Americans, they always use the language of ghostliness," she wrote. "They insist that Indians are able to appear and disappear suddenly and mysteriously, and also that they are ultimately doomed to vanish."

In that respect, Indians are not alone. The identities of the men who made ghosts of the Conestogas also vanished without a trace, thanks to a decision by their community, county and colony to keep their secret forever.

CHAPTER 12

"They Had Possession and Would Keep It"

Why did the unidentified vigilantes from Paxton kill the Conestogas? Of several motivating factors, one of the most obvious was revenge. Revenge has been the driving force behind many massacres, including the assault on the undefended South Vietnamese hamlet of My Lai in 1968. At My Lai, American soldiers systematically slaughtered several hundred civilians, almost all of them women, children and old men.

The army eventually brought criminal charges against sixteen soldiers, finding only Lieutenant William Calley Jr. guilty. During the trial, Staff Sergeant Kenneth Hodges testified about the military briefing provided by his company commander before the soldiers entered the village. "This was a time for us to get even," he said. "A time to settle the score. A time for revenge—when we can get revenge for our fallen comrades. The order we were given was to kill and destroy everything that was in the village."

No one knows if anyone gave orders when the Paxton Rangers attacked the Conestogas, but the method of operations seems to have been the same as at My Lai. This was the Rangers' time to get even, to settle the score by killing, burning and looting. The Rangers' elemental rage, what caused them to blow heads apart and hack off body parts, must have come from a deep-rooted need to exact revenge for similar mutilations committed by Indians.

The Rangers also may have acted out of fear that Pontiac's forces would continue to overrun Pennsylvania settlements until they reached Paxton. They may have thought that killing noncombatants would transmit to enemy Indians some of the fear and intimidation that the whole frontier felt during an uprising that targeted unsuspecting white settlers as well as fortified soldiers.

The Rangers also likely killed the Conestogas because they were frustrated by their failed upriver expeditions and saw an easy opportunity to attack Indians at home. British Colonel Henry Bouquet criticized the Rangers for this in a letter to John Harris in July 1764. "Will not People Say that they have found it easier to kill Indians in a Goal," he wrote, "than to fight them fairly in the Woods?" Or, as Lancaster historian John W.W. Loose has said, "Why run out to western Pennsylvania when you can kill them locally?" After seeing what Indians could do to fellow militiamen and Connecticut settlers, the Rangers were not concerned about fighting "fairly" or in distinguishing Indian foe from Indian friend or neutral Indian. They simply wanted to kill Indians.[31]

The Rangers' motivations were more complex, of course. They also thought they were executing real or potential spies for hostile Indians and sending a warning shot to Pennsylvania authorities that the frontier wanted more attention paid to its concerns. And they had even more motives.

Fully understanding the reasons for the fierce attacks at Conestoga and Lancaster requires a closer look at the Rangers' ethnic and religious background, where they came from and where they settled.

In the seventeenth century, thousands of Scottish Presbyterians moved to the north of Ireland, mainly to the province of Ulster. Britain's Queen Elizabeth I called these people "the wild Irish" because of their independent and combative spirit cultivated during hundreds of years of border strife with England, France and Ireland.

In the eighteenth century, their descendants—referred to generally as Scots-Irish but identifying themselves primarily with Scotland—came to America. Many eventually settled on the Pennsylvania frontier. By 1760, nearly one of every five Lancaster County residents was Scots-Irish.

Unlike the English and many Germans, who had the means to move into the settled areas of the colony, the Scots-Irish generally moved to the frontier and served as a buffer against Indians. Many resented being treated as if they were a marginal group. That resentment is clear in the "Declaration" and "Remonstrance" they delivered at Germantown in 1764.

An old joke claims the Scots-Irish were brewed in Scotland, bottled in Ireland and uncorked in America. It might be said that men who were proud to descend from rebellious and often victorious forbears uncorked their frustration at being considered second-class citizens in the faces of the Indians they would displace.

The first Scots-Irish settlers arrived at Paxton when Lenapes still controlled the area and used it as a major trading center. A large influx of Scots-Irish and German settlers drove out the last of the Indians by the 1720s. Many of the newcomers squatted illegally on land that had been cleared by the original inhabitants. Clannish by nature, they formed a close-knit cluster.

If these settlers gave much thought to what they were doing, beyond making homes for their families, they probably congratulated themselves for shoving the barbarians out of the way. Most Scots-Irish were Presbyterians, and many Presbyterians thought Indians were heathens who had to be eradicated so that believers could possess the land. John Elder and other Presbyterian ministers spoke directly to that attitude when they quoted from Deuteronomy 7:2: "And when the Lord thy God shall deliver them before thee: thou shalt smite them, and utterly destroy them; thou shalt make no covenant with them, nor shew mercy unto them."

The Presbyterian settlers of Paxton understood that they were part of God's plan to displace unbelievers, but they had no plan of their own for creating a defined place to live. Paxton never developed a town center or a real government; the community was composed of individuals with a common ethnic background and religious affiliation living independently in the same vicinity. With a church preaching against "the heathen" and no local government to sanction them, the Rangers felt little restraint when they went hunting for the scalps of any and all Indians.

"Paxton was a product of political, social and economic attitudes that were individualistic at the expense of community solidarity," George Franz explained in his study of Paxton. "In reaction to specific crises, residents, both temporary and permanent, consistently called for immediate, extemporaneous responses which were often extra-legal and outside the structure of established government."

Paxton's strategic location on the Susquehanna made it a tempting target. After enduring a severe Indian attack early in the French and Indian War, Paxtonians were determined not to allow a repeat during Pontiac's Rebellion five years later. The commonwealth had authorized Elder and his militia to protect Lancaster County—nothing more. Nevertheless, the Rangers decided to take the war to the Indians on the West Branch of the Susquehanna in August 1763.

Governor Hamilton rebuked them for that foray in a letter to Timothy Horsfield, a justice of the peace in Northampton County:

> *These are a most unaccountable, headstrong people and have no authority from me for what they are doing; on the contrary, had I known of their intentions sooner, I would have endeavored to put it under the direction of some persons on whose prudence I could have relied...They are certainly doing a very illegal and unjustifiable thing and what, in more quiet and settled times would subject them to grevious punishment.*

Hamilton also opposed the October journey up the North Branch because he feared the Rangers would kill friendly Indians there. He told Horsfield that it would not long be possible to keep the Paxton men from killing Indians, "whether friends or foes."

And so the next two Ranger campaigns, to Conestoga and Lancaster two months later, must have come as no real surprise to the government or to anyone else who understood why the Rangers believed in waging total war against their enemies.

Following the massacre, the Rangers fervently endorsed the list of grievances in the "Remonstrance" they presented at Philadelphia. These reasoned arguments seemed to add legitimacy to their killing spree in Lancaster. The Rangers really believed they lacked equal representation in Pennsylvania's government; they really believed government should do more to repress Indians and protect frontier settlers.

But there were forces at work beyond a desire to protect home and hearth by awakening a Quaker-ruled government to the realities of frontier life. There was a distinct feeling among these proud descendants of Scottish warriors that Indians were inferior beings who seemed to be getting a better deal than they.

The Rangers resented the Indians at Conestoga because they received government aid while the Rangers' own families fended for themselves under constant fear of attack. They despised these Indians because, although they were as red as hostile Indians, government officials, particularly Quakers, treated them as if they were the equal of poor white settlers. And they envied the Conestogas' four hundred acres of fertile Manor Township land—far more and better land, per individual, than most Scots-Irish settlers had.

Throughout their "Declaration" and "Remonstrance," the Paxton Boys declared their hatred for the government's aid to the Conestogas while white settlers went wanting. Furthermore, they believed the Quaker-dominated government had relegated them to be "Dupes and Slaves to Indians."

In the "Declaration," the Paxton Boys discussed this complaint in reference to the 1762 treaty negotiated in Lancaster. First they said they resented the "exorbitant Presents, and great Servility therein paid to *Indians*" in previous treaties. Then they blasted the Lancaster treaty for not addressing the issues of murdered and captive settlers but "concluding Friendship with the *Indians* and allowing them a plenteous Trade of all kinds of Commodities."

This presumed deference to Indians on the part of a Quaker-run government was bad enough in itself to the Scots-Irish Rangers, but the fact that the Indians were not white made it worse. Visceral racism, as we understand it today, did not exist in 1760s America, but Indians and white settlers were becoming acutely aware of their physical differences. Franklin made that clear in his *Narrative* when he said the Rangers were operating on the basis of skin and hair color when they killed the Conestogas.

John Elder, who called Africans "the Progeny of Ham" and kept a man who was either a slave or an indentured servant, almost certainly considered Indians as inferior as black slaves. Similarly, members of Elder's congregation would have believed themselves superior to all red men, whether they were hostile Iroquois warriors upriver or peaceful Indians at Conestoga.[32]

But what galled the Paxtonians as much as or more than anything else was the inescapable reality that these inferior beings lived on some of the best unsettled land in Lancaster County, land that the Rangers believed they could have used more productively.

The Scots-Irish way of dealing with land they wanted had little to do with the law. If they could not obtain property through legitimate purchases, they simply took it. A number of immigrants had settled illegally on Penn's old Conestoga Manor in the 1720s and 1730s. At that time, the manor still contained some sixteen thousand acres, including the four hundred-plus where the Indians lived. The squatters began building their own cabins near the four hundred acres, which restricted Indian hunting and other movement throughout the larger tract.

In December 1730, James Logan told Thomas Penn that a "panel of Disorderly People" from the Scots-Irish communities of Donegal and Swatara had taken over Conestoga Manor. "This is the most audacious attack that has ever yet been offer'd," he wrote. Logan asked the magistrates and sheriff of Lancaster County and a militia organized by Donegal Presbyterian Church to evict the intruders and destroy their homes. The authorities burned thirty cabins. But then Logan's successor, Richard Peters, had to evict another wave of Scots-Irish squatters. And some of these people quickly returned and built new cabins, only to be burned out again.

Meanwhile, German farmers, generally wealthier than the Scots-Irish, were squatting nearby. The government eventually permitted these German

Mennonites to purchase the land they had claimed originally without deeds. The evicted Scots-Irish, who moved north to Donegal, Paxton, Derry and beyond, did not forget this discrimination.

By the late 1730s, German farmers had settled on much of the sixteen thousand acres, nearly surrounding the Conestogas. Michael Baughman, a Swiss Mennonite who had purchased other Conestoga Manor lands from the Penns and resold them to his friends, petitioned the commonwealth in 1739 to "purchase the spot where the old Indian Town stands with the whole vacancy."

Logan rejected Baughman's request, not only because of the 1701 treaty that granted the land to the Indians but also because he believed it was advantageous to maintain Indians within the white settlement as an example of the government's beneficence to other Indians. Also, the Indians served as a listening post: by another article in that treaty, the Conestogas had pledged to inform the Penns if they heard any threats made against the English by "evil minded persons and sowers of sedition."

Lancaster County's Scots-Irish Presbyterians and German Mennonites were not alone in coveting Indian land. Well-watered lands with superior soil that had been cleared for cabins and gardens appealed to many settlers. Dozens of early Pennsylvania towns, including Paxton, grew up on "Indian old fields," as they were known. But Conestoga Indian Town remained off limits.[33]

Appropriating Indian land, by squatting or simply farming over the boundary line, as some of the Conestogas' neighbors increasingly did, was an individual's way of doing what government did continuously and more broadly by treaty or proclamation. The purpose of almost every treaty, from the British point of view, was to push the frontier farther west to accommodate an accelerating influx of settlers.[34]

The Paxton Rangers' reasons for wiping out the Conestogas—down to the last child who might have inherited Indian Town—were more pointed. They killed the inhabitants of Indian Town, as Robert Proud put it, so that they "might possess the land alone."

Following the massacre, the Paxtonians tried to possess the land in short order. They cited "the right of conquest"—a vigilante version of the proposition, accepted until the early twentieth century, that a victorious nation can claim ownership of conquered territory.[35]

The Penns actually had owned the four hundred acres at Indian Town since the treaty of 1701. They maintained control after the murder of the Conestogas. The land's management devolved upon Sir William Johnson, superintendent of Indian Affairs in North America. Johnson appointed Jacob Whisler, a Mennonite neighbor, as caretaker.

On March 12, 1764—less than three months after the Rangers burned Indian Town—Whisler wrote an urgent note to Surveyor General William Peters. He said two men had come to his home and informed him that nine or ten families intended to take possession of the fifty acres of cleared land at Indian Town by right of conquest.

In early April, Whisler wrote again saying two families were already living on the land and a third was plowing it. The caretaker took some neighbors with him to warn the squatters to leave. "The answer was that they had Possession and would keep it and would Loose their Lives before they would be turned off the Land," Whisler reported. "They Care for no Governour, Sheriff nor any other officers untill they Cann peaceable go on there own Lands again to Settle and will allow no Other Person or Persons to Settle there without themselves." Whisler identified the two families as those of Richard Meloon and Robert Bow. He said Bow "is related to the Scotts families in Donegal."

Edward Shippen reported to Governor Penn about the same time that settlers were building new log houses on the Indian land and that an elderly couple named Magginty was "living in an Indian Wigwam."

Men identified as coming directly from Paxton also began building on this land and apparently stayed well after the spring of 1764. In January 1766, Whisler complained to Chief Justice William Allen that Robert Poke, a Paxton man who had moved onto the land shortly after the massacre, had obtained a keg of liquor that he intended to share with a group of his fellow Paxtonians.

Anticipating trouble, Whisler and an assistant went to the house of Thomas Fisher, who had been helping Whisler manage the property. There they found "a large Company of Men with Horses being about 25 or 30... many of them having poweder Horns and pouches and some of them Guns." A long argument ensued about who actually owned the land. Robert Poke was involved and also a man named Bayley. The Paxton contingent said that neither Whisler nor Pennsylvania's proprietors "had any right to that Land, but that it belonged to the Indians that were killed and that [the Paxton men] had now the best right to it, and would have it and keep it in spite of the Governor & Proprietors."

But the Paxton men did not keep it; neither did Jacob Whisler. Someone else—someone not associated with Paxton or Donegal and not a Scots-Irish Presbyterian—eventually turned the tract into his personal wheat field and apple orchard. Indian Town was his reward for a church service well timed and a literary hatchet job well done.

CHAPTER 13

"Eternal Shame & Reproach"

In the comic film *Grosse Point Blank*, a hired assassin repeatedly shifts responsibility for his hits to his employers. "It's not me," the assassin insists. The act of pulling the trigger, he suggests, is of little consequence compared with the directive to pull the trigger.

Just so, the Paxton Rangers might have pointed to those who encouraged and/or enabled them to kill the Conestogas. "It wasn't us," they might have said, if they had been brought to trial. "We took our marching orders for Conestoga Indian Town from _____ and _____. The men who called the shots at the Lancaster workhouse were _____ and _____."

Filling in those blanks is relatively easy compared to naming members of the actual assassination squads.

There is no difficulty with the Conestoga massacre. As the Rangers' spiritual adviser and military commander, John Elder bears primary responsibility. Elder may have never literally told the Rangers to kill noncombatants and burn their village, but as the pastor/commander who continually urged the Rangers to liquidate the heathen from the face of the earth, he inflamed his militia and provided its members with all the rhetorical authority they needed to act. Elder knew what the Rangers planned to do, failed to stop them and failed to alert authorities in Lancaster. And when it was finished, Elder protected the killers by refusing to identify any of them, though many sat in Paxton Presbyterian's pews.

As Elder's close friend and parishioner, and the generally recognized political leader of the Paxton community, John Harris Jr. most likely helped fan the flames. Harris had turned his home into a fort during the French and Indian War. He decried the "General Pannick & Confusion Prevailing among the whole Countrey" as Pontiac's Rebellion heated up. He had little respect for the Conestogas, referring to them in one letter as the "Basket & Broommaking Bandittey."

Peter Seibert believes that Harris and Elder may well have believed that, with the Conestogas out of the way, central Pennsylvania would seem more peaceful and Paxton would flourish. As two of the largest landholders in Paxton—Harris owned the land along the river and Elder owned large lots just inland—the community leaders had reason to want to protect their investment. "This area needed to be settled," Seibert explains. "Getting rid of the Indians became a driving force."

There is no evidence that Elder and Harris encouraged the second attack. If they did, they surely had to rely on others, closer to the scene, to prepare for it. Unlike the dawn attack on a sleeping rural village, the successful assault on a government building in the center of a bustling town in broad daylight required advance planning. Some, at the time, suggested that it required a conspiracy.

Consider again what occurred on the afternoon of December 27, 1763.

After indicating that they would attack a second time, the Paxton Rangers rode boldly into Lancaster on a Tuesday afternoon. They arrived just as many of the town's leaders had settled into the pews of St. James Episcopal for a delayed Christmas service. They parked their horses at Matthias Slough's tavern on Centre Square, and Slough had to hurry to beat the Rangers as they strode purposefully down icy King Street to the Prince Street workhouse. The prison keeper, Felix Donnally, had left the premises. Sheriff John Hay, apparently the only guard posted that afternoon, quickly stepped aside, as did the late-arriving Slough. The Rangers entered the workhouse and slaughtered the Indians. Then they returned to Slough's, mounted their horses, rode around the county courthouse to celebrate their accomplishment and left town unmolested.

This unchallenged assault prompts several questions.

Was it by chance that the Rangers struck in the middle of an afternoon of a business day, rather than at night when an attack might more logically have been anticipated and, in fact, had been guarded against on previous occasions? Was it a coincidence that many of the town's leaders, including the county's chief magistrate and the town's chief burgess, were attending a church service during the attack? Why was the sheriff alone guarding the workhouse? Where was the jailor? Where were other local guards? Where was Captain Robertson's regiment? Would the Rangers have separated themselves from their horses if they had anticipated resistance and a need to get away quickly? Why did the Rangers believe they could thumb their noses with impunity at the government and the town by riding around the courthouse and cheering after the assault?

Most early chroniclers had little difficulty answering these questions. They concluded that Lancaster residents had enabled the killings—either by assuring the raiders that no one would stop them and by providing easy entrance to the workhouse, by passively sequestering themselves in a church or by watching fearfully from behind windows as up to one hundred vigilantes armed to the teeth strode through town.

Quakers were especially incensed by what they viewed as a conspiratorial, or even collective, decision to massacre the Conestogas. "Abettors" was their operative word. The author of one of the earliest pamphlets opposing the Paxton Rangers condemned "these People and their Abettors" for making conditions on the frontier less safe by killing peaceful Indians. In Philadelphia, speaking to the provincial council, Isaac Norris damned the "Persons who perpetrated such shocking Barbarities in Lancaster County, and their Abettors." In Lancaster, David Henderson railed against "those murderers & their abettors."

A sizeable number of "abettors" may have assisted the killers.

Jailor Felix Donnally, fearing trouble, sent his family away from the jail and then, unaccountably, disappeared himself on the day of the assault. His actions may have had something to do with his lack of experience: he had been appointed jailor in November. Or he may have deliberately walked away from an attack in force that he knew he could not and perhaps did not want to stop.

The sheriff and coroner, charged by their elected offices to uphold the law, became culpable by stepping aside when the vigilantes appeared at the workhouse. John Hay, whose term as sheriff was nearing its end, said Slough and he had no choice "without Danger of Life"—a submissive attitude that does not mesh with his responsibility to protect Indians under the care of both Lancaster County and Pennsylvania.[36]

And it is curious that the coroner, Matthias Slough, was at his inn when the Rangers arrived instead of attending the Christmas service at St. James. Such church services were not optional in those days; a community leader was bound to be there. Instead, Slough watched the Rangers stable their horses at his inn, raced to the workhouse, allowed the militiamen to kill its inmates and then directed removal of the bodies.

The German innkeeper and dry-goods merchant was one of the wealthiest landholders and the largest slaveholder in town. He had just turned thirty at the time of the massacre, but Slough already served the county as both coroner and treasurer and the town as a burgess. A master politician as well as businessman, he may have believed he had nothing to gain by opposing an armed band of vigilantes representing a large voting bloc.

But Slough was not named among several officials accused of conspiracy in Jacob Mombert's 1869 history of Lancaster County. Mombert cited a statement made by John Reynolds in the *Lancaster Journal*, which Reynolds edited from 1820 to 1834:

> *It is a little remarkable that three of the persons who were most deeply concerned in the murder of the Indians at Lancaster, William Hays* [sic], *the Sheriff; and two persons of the name of Smith and Howard, met with an untimely fate; Hays was killed in a Saw Mill, Smith drowned himself, and Howard fell on a knife, which he had in his hand, by accident, which caused his death. Wm. Hays Jr.,* [sic] *the son of the Sheriff, and Donnelly* [sic] *the jailor, were also suspected of being in the plot.*

It is difficult to know what to make of this statement about men who were "deeply concerned in the murder" meeting an untimely fate. But Reynolds, of Irish lineage and the father of Union General John Fulton Reynolds, should be accepted as a reliable source that Hay and Donnally were prime suspects in a "plot" to raid the workhouse and kill the Indians.

None of these people was a primary abettor, however. The jailor, sheriff and coroner did not control what happened that afternoon. The Conestogas, as Governor Penn acknowledged, were "under the immediate Care and Protection of the Magistrates." Anyone searching for the chief enabler of a conspiracy to kill the Indians should look to the magistrates first.

Many early critics condemned the magistrates for not employing Robertson's Highlanders or other guards to protect Indians they knew were vulnerable to a second attack. A week after the massacre, Pennsylvania assemblyman Samuel Foulke said the magistrates deserved "Eternal Shame & reproach." In early March 1764, Philadelphia merchant James Pemberton told a Quaker friend in London that he was disturbed by the "Supineness of the Magistrates in Lancaster in omitting proper measures to prevent the murder of the Indians in that Burrough."A year later, surveyor Charles Mason found it "strange" that Lancaster "never offered to oppose" the killers. Early historian Robert Proud blamed the murder of the Conestogas on "the connivance, if not the encouragement, of the *Christian-professing Magistrates*, and other principal persons of that town."

Some observers criticized both the magistrates and the governor for ignoring the Paxton Boys' crimes and thereby contributing to widespread disrespect for the law. The Pennsylvania Assembly continued this drumbeat throughout the 1760s.

In 1768, for example, the assembly attacked John Penn after Frederick Stump, who had killed and scalped ten Indians in Cumberland County, was freed from jail by a frontier mob. In a bitter exchange of letters, published in the *Minutes of the Provincial Council*, the assembly demanded that Penn reissue his proclamation against the Conestogas' killers, increase the reward for their capture and call witnesses to Philadelphia. Penn refused.

Assembly Quakers charged that Penn had set the stage for Stump's atrocity and other attacks on Indians by not following through on strongly worded proclamations issued after the Conestoga massacres and by not removing Lancaster's magistrates, sheriff and coroner because of their "unparalleled Inactivity." They questioned Penn: "Can it appear possible to a rational Mind, if the Magistrates had exerted their Authority when the Offence was Committed, or at any Time since, that the Perpetrators of so flagrant a Crime, in so public a Manner, cou'd remain undiscovered, and Elude the Efforts of Justice?"[37]

The most prominent of Lancaster County's magistrates, sixty-year-old Edward Shippen, had sat comfortably in his pew at St. James as the Paxton Rangers rode uncontested into town. Afterward, Shippen would write late into the night trying to explain away the magistrates' responsibility for the slaughter. His story seems to have played well with Penn, but it doesn't square with what actually occurred.

Compare the Lancaster magistrates' passive response to a known hostile threat from the Paxton Rangers to Philadelphia's militant and effective reaction to the approach of the Paxton Boys. The difference in attitude and action is striking, although, of course, Philadelphians had the benefit of knowing the mayhem the men from Paxton were capable of causing.

It seems possible, perhaps even probable, that Shippen and his fellow magistrates not only did little or nothing to discourage the attack but also actively prepared the way, purposely limiting the guard at the workhouse while using the Reverend Thomas Barton's church service to provide cover for themselves.

The Rangers knew that their community's leaders—Elder and Harris—were in constant contact with Shippen. When would-be lawbreakers know they have the county's top judge on their side, they might act boldly by separating themselves from their horses, killing and scalping "protected" Indians and riding rings around the courthouse.

Edward Shippen was one of the most formidable men in eighteenth-century Pennsylvania.[38] He made much of his money buying furs from Indian traders and consigning them to British merchants. Meanwhile, he acquired considerable real estate in Philadelphia, Lancaster and Shippensburg, which he laid out and named for himself in 1733. James Hamilton appointed Shippen as his land agent in Lancaster. Shippen depended on Indian traders for fur sales and on Indian peace for land sales.

Trained as a lawyer, Shippen maintained a lifelong love of books and learning, which he put to practical use as a founder and trustee of the College of New Jersey (Princeton) and a founder of one of the colony's first subscription libraries in Lancaster.

Shippen held many of the municipal and county offices available in Philadelphia and Lancaster. He began as a Philadelphia councilman in 1732, became a city alderman in 1743 and served as mayor from 1744 to 1745. He also was appointed a justice of the peace of Philadelphia County. At the same time, he acquired appointed offices in Lancaster County, which he administered during occasional fur-buying expeditions. He became clerk of the county's Court of Quarter Sessions of Peace in 1737. Eight years later, he took over as Register of Deeds and Prothonotary.

In 1752, Shippen moved permanently to Lancaster County, not so that he could more efficiently conduct his various county offices at close range, but to escape a difficult social situation in Philadelphia. In 1743, eight years after the death of his first wife, Shippen married Mary Nowland. Mrs. Nowland had assumed that her first husband had died in Barbados, but the man surfaced several weeks after the Shippen–Nowland nuptials. A Philadelphia grand jury indicted the Shippens for bigamy. To avoid punishment, the two lived in separate homes until Nowland actually died, but given all the gossip of nine years, life together in Philadelphia thereafter seemed impossible.

When big-fish Shippen moved to medium-pond Lancaster, he retained much of the influence he had gained with Pennsylvania officials in Philadelphia. His family connections to the government alone were extensive. Two of Shippen's sons, Edward IV and Joseph, held provincial offices with considerable authority. Chief Justice William Allen was the first cousin of Shippen's first wife. When Edward Shippen spoke, official Philadelphia generally listened.

Shippen's opinion of Indians deteriorated when he moved closer to the frontier, especially as the French and Indian War and then Pontiac's

Rebellion unnerved white settlers, ruined trade with Indians and undermined interest in purchasing land. As a Presbyterian, Shippen subscribed to John Elder's opinion of the heathen natives. He not only despised hostile Indians but also ascribed to them a strength they never possessed. Writing to son Joseph in June 1763, Shippen said Pontiac's forces had "a deep plan for the extermination of us all."[39]

Shippen's letters to Governor Hamilton, John Elder and his sons during the summer and autumn of 1763 exhibit an intense interest in and considerable knowledge of Indian movements. That September, he excitedly informed Joseph that the Paxton Rangers were preparing to strike up the West Branch to defeat the "naked, black painted serpents on their own Dunhil." Repeatedly, Shippen referred to the importance of protecting Lancaster County's northern townships as an outer defense for the town of Lancaster. On October 29, 1763, he told Hamilton that the government should reinforce Elder "or that little garrison will be cut off, the Consequences of which would be the total Evacuation of Paxton, Derry and Hanover Townships."

Shippen remained in close contact with Elder throughout the period, but he did not necessarily obtain all of his information about the Paxton Rangers from him. Shippen's opinion, relayed to Elder two days after the first massacre, that the Rangers were "resolved to justify the action" must have come from an independent source close to the militiamen.

While there is absolutely no evidence that Shippen invited the Rangers to attack the workhouse, there are multiple indications that he may have set the stage for the assault and was eager to let it pass without punishing the perpetrators.

It was Shippen who ordered the fourteen remaining Conestogas to the workhouse where they might be secured, not only to protect them from further attacks by the vigilantes, but also to protect the community from any reprisal by the Indians; it was Shippen who ordered a report on rumors that the Rangers were preparing for another attack and then decided that one night's investigation was sufficient to discount the idea; it was Shippen who claimed he was not aware that hundreds of Captain Robertson's Highlanders were billeted in a town of two thousand residents; it was Shippen who must have been aware of the meager guard at the workhouse during daylight hours on December 27; it was Shippen who provided a seemingly solid alibi by sitting inside St. James during the slaughter; it was Shippen who failed to order an inquest into the second massacre; it was Shippen who ignored John Penn's repeated requests to identify, arrest and try the killers; it was Shippen who instead authorized the collecting of affidavits against the dead Conestogas; and it was Shippen who ultimately let the Paxton Rangers get away with murder.

As chief magistrate and foremost citizen of Lancaster County, a man with the ear of Pennsylvania's governor, chief justice and key legislators, Shippen exercised near total control of Lancaster in 1763. The Paxton Rangers could not have gone free without his blessing.

But Edward Shippen could not do everything. He needed help.

Thomas Barton eventually was paid handsomely for that help by replacing Jacob Whisler, Indian Town's manager. It seems possible, perhaps even probable, that the minister received the coveted prize as a lifetime grant because he helped to facilitate the workhouse massacre and then defended the murderers in print.

Barton was nearly forty years old in 1768 and increasingly concerned about living in Lancaster on a minister's wages with an expanding family. Grain was expensive in the town, Barton told Sir William Johnson, with whom he regularly corresponded. The minister said he hoped to grow enough wheat on the old Indian lands to keep his family in bread for the year.

But others, including Paxton squatters and the Iroquois, already had claimed that land. Why did Barton get it?

The reason generally provided is that the minister had just spent considerable effort trying to educate Johnson's teenage son, and that Johnson provided the land in return. This may be only partially true.

William of Canajoharie, also known as Tagchenuto, was a son of Johnson's first Mohawk wife, who disappeared. The single father had other things to do besides instruct the young man, so he sent him to Barton, a fellow native of Ireland whose teaching abilities he respected. William arrived in Lancaster in the summer of 1767, and everything went well for several months. But the situation deteriorated in the winter of 1768, at least in part because anti-Indian sentiment in the town increasingly repelled a prideful teenager who had been raised as the son of an important white man. William asked to return to Johnson's estate in New York and did. Barton asked to manage Indian Town and did.

But in a December 1770 letter he wrote to Edmund Physick, the Penns' land agent, Barton suggested that taking over the land was not his idea or Johnson's. He said "some of my friends" made that decision. "And the thing being mentioned to the Governor, he was pleased to consent to my occupying it as Whisler had done."

Whether he came to occupy the land through William Johnson or after friends interceded with the governor, Barton found he had a big job on his hands. He told Physick that the fifty acres of cleared land "was much out of order. The fences were mostly gone to decay. It had neither house, Barn, nor Stable, except *two Cabbins erected by the Paxton People*." Barton constructed a barn, planted an apple orchard and fenced in a garden. Developing the tract was a time-consuming task that he welcomed as a relief from demanding ministerial duties. It was his land, and he was determined to put his imprint on it.

There is another theory as to why Barton took over at Indian Town. It suggests that the land was the minister's compensation for writing *The Conduct of the Paxton-Men*, the 1764 pamphlet that rebutted Benjamin Franklin's *A Narrative of the Late Massacres*.

James P. Myers Jr., a Gettysburg College historian, spent considerable time examining Barton's writings. Myers seems to have established, beyond doubt, Barton's authorship of the pro–Paxton Boys pamphlet, even though the writing contradicts other statements Barton made against the massacre and in sympathy for Christianized Indians.[40]

Myers explained in a 1994 *Pennsylvania History* article that a number of influential people responded to Barton's financial distress and desire to leave Lancaster in the late 1760s by providing for his welfare. The London-based Society for the Propagation of the Gospel in Foreign Parts (SPG), which sponsored his missionary work in America, increased his annual allowance. Thomas Penn offered him fifty pounds. And then he got Indian Town.

"Because of his established value to Church and Proprietary and perhaps because of what he had achieved in writing *The Conduct of the Paxton-Men*," Myers wrote, "the S.P.G., Thomas Penn, and Sir William Johnson handsomely rewarded Barton and obtained thereby his agreement to remain in Lancaster."[41] Myers went further. He said Barton wrote the pamphlet "under some kind of pressure, or even coercion…Although it is improbable that the Penns and their leading supporters were pressuring him, people lower down, say, the Shippens or other officials in Lancaster, probably looked to him to respond to Franklin's *Narrative*."

The amount of effort Barton spent defending the magistrates in his tract suggests that his parishioner and good friend, Edward Shippen, may have put him up to it or perhaps was reading over his shoulder. The Lancaster massacre, Barton asserted and reasserted, was not the result of "any Misconduct of the Magistrates."

Barton indicated, as had Elder and Shippen, that he had talked with men who had ridden with the killers. He declared that he knew Franklin erred when he contended that the Conestogas had died on their knees pleading their innocence because "no one had any Kind of Intercourse with them, nor even saw them during that Time, except those that killed them, and they declare, that no one of them appeared in that Posture, nor spoke a Word."

How could this well-known cleric of the Church of England be pressured into defending murderers, even to the point of contradicting Franklin's argument by accepting the Rangers' description of the Conestogas' death? A strong possibility once again: money. Barton had too few pounds and too many children. This was true early in his career, and the problem grew as he aged.

Barton had left Ireland for Philadelphia in the early 1750s. There he taught school and married Esther Rittenhouse, sister of the botanist David Rittenhouse. She would bear him eight children, a sizeable brood to raise on a minister's salary. Barton returned to Great Britain to take divine orders as a minister and came back to America as an itinerant SPG missionary. He settled first in Huntingdon, Adams County, and rode a circuit to Carlisle and York. He said his goals were to expand Anglican influence, construct new churches and convert Indians before French-allied Catholic missionaries could get to them.

The French and Indian War stirred Barton to action. He published a popular sermon, *Unanimity and Public Spirit*, urging all Anglicans and dissenters to unite against a common foe. Along with many ministers at the time, he also participated in the military effort. He organized his Anglican parishioners into military units and coordinated a defense strategy with his Scots-Irish neighbors. As Anglican chaplain-at-large during the Forbes campaign to seize Fort Duquesne, he prayed with men who went into battle with Indians. Several years later he even considered leaving the SPG and starting a military career.[42]

Barton moved to Lancaster in 1759, after attacks to the east of the Susquehanna River had all but ended.[43] His primary church was St. James, but he also served parishes in nearby Pequea and Churchtown. He had plans to create a school in Lancaster for Indian, black and poor children, and he wanted to establish a mission among the Indians. Although his war experience had fostered a hatred for hostiles, he remained dedicated to the education, religious and otherwise, of Christianized Indians.

Pontiac's Rebellion ruined Barton's plan to spend several months in Indian territory, learning the language and laying a foundation for future missionary work. He shared the bitterness of his parishioners as he watched the frontier once again erupt in flames. "The Barbarians have renewed their Hostilities against us, and our Country bleeds again under the Savage knife!" he wrote to the SPG in late June 1763. "The dreadful News of Murdering,

Burning and Scalping is daily conveyed to us, and confirmed with shocking additions." And he further asserted that "one half of the Inhabitants will be massacred before any proper relief can be obtained for them."

Barton supported a proposed Scalp Act that summer because young men who might not enlist otherwise "would be prompted by Revenge, Duty, Ambition & the Prospect of Reward to carry Fire & Sword into the Heart of the Indian Country." The minister believed the practice could "put a final stop to those Barbarians." But the Scalp Act failed to gain passage; scalp bounties were not authorized until a year later.

Once he got rolling with his anti-Indian rhetoric, Barton may have begun to wonder if the Conestogas indeed served as spies for Pontiac's forces. From there, it is not so large a leap to believe that the sometime militant minister would be willing to help sell out the Conestogas.[44]

The timing of the massacre, while Barton was presiding over a delayed Christmas service at St. James, can hardly be coincidental. Under ordinary circumstances, Barton's parishioners in Lancaster might have expected him to hold that service at St. James on Christmas Day. Instead, he conducted the December 25 service in Pequea—a small village eighteen miles south of Lancaster—and presumably rode to Churchtown—twenty miles east of Lancaster—the following day. That left Lancaster for December 27.

St. James's historian, Leo Shelley, says the Pequea and Churchtown congregations were substantial, so he does not find it particularly unusual that Barton would relegate St. James's service to last place in order. But the timing of the service is not so important as the question of whether the Rangers took advantage of it to attack the town or whether a representative of St. James invited the Rangers to attack at that hour.

It is difficult to imagine the Rangers telling St. James's elders to schedule a church service at 2:00 p.m. on December 27 so that they could assault the Conestogas in the workhouse. The service likely was scheduled well before the Conestogas moved into Lancaster.

It is less difficult to imagine Barton or another representative of St. James telling a Ranger that the town's leading authorities would be occupied at the hour of service, providing a perfect time for an assault on the workhouse as well as a perfect excuse for inaction by those who were piously occupied.

Did Barton preside over a church service during which the Conestogas were murdered and then write a diatribe against the Indians only for a promise of a future land payoff? James Myers suggested there was something more prompting him. "It is likely that some powerful figures discovered a way to undermine his scruples," Myers wrote. "Possibly he yielded to dire economic need, together with the promise of immediate financial remuneration, or even to threats to divulge publicly an earlier misdeed…or to both of these."

One earlier misdeed, Myers explained in a 1995 *Pennsylvania Magazine of History & Biography* article, involved plagiarizing much of *Unanimity and Public Spirit* in 1755. Critics tore into Barton when they discovered the literary theft, but Pennsylvania's proprietary interests defended him because the propagandist publication helped to unite English colonists against a common foe. The proprietors effectively silenced the critics but perhaps retained the option to reintroduce Barton's transgression at a later date.

That Barton did yield to powerful figures—possibly in coordinating the massacre with his Christmas service and probably in his defense of the murderers in the anti-Franklin pamphlet—seems evident. That these powerful figures helped Barton to obtain Indian Town in exchange for this help seems even more clear.

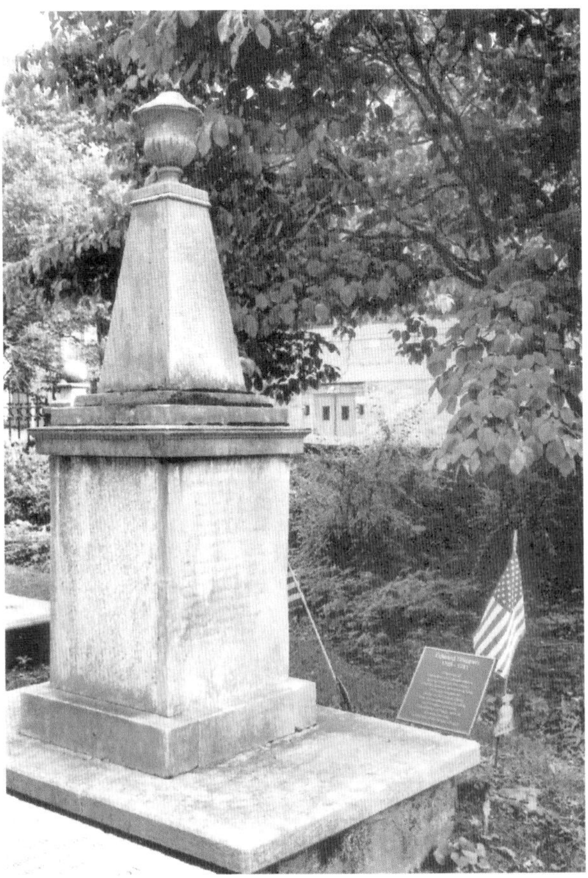

Chief Magistrate Edward Shippen's tombstone and memorial plaque in the cemetery of St. James Episcopal Church. *Photo by the author.*

But most biographers slide by all of this to concentrate on Barton's affairs during the Revolution. While the leading men of St. James—Shippen, Slough, George Ross, William Atlee, Jasper Yeates and others—became revolutionaries, Barton remained as loyal to the crown in 1776 as he had to the proprietary interests in 1763–64. The minister continued to include prayers for King George III in his service. Rebellious parishioners desired otherwise. So Barton closed the church after independence was declared in the summer of 1776. After refusing to take the oath of allegiance to Pennsylvania, he moved to British-occupied New York two years later.

In 1780, at age fifty, Thomas Barton died and was buried in New York City.

Edward Shippen died in Lancaster the following year, at age seventy-eight. He is buried among other Revolutionary Patriots and not far from a memorial stone to Barton beneath a magnificent sycamore in St. James's lovingly landscaped cemetery.

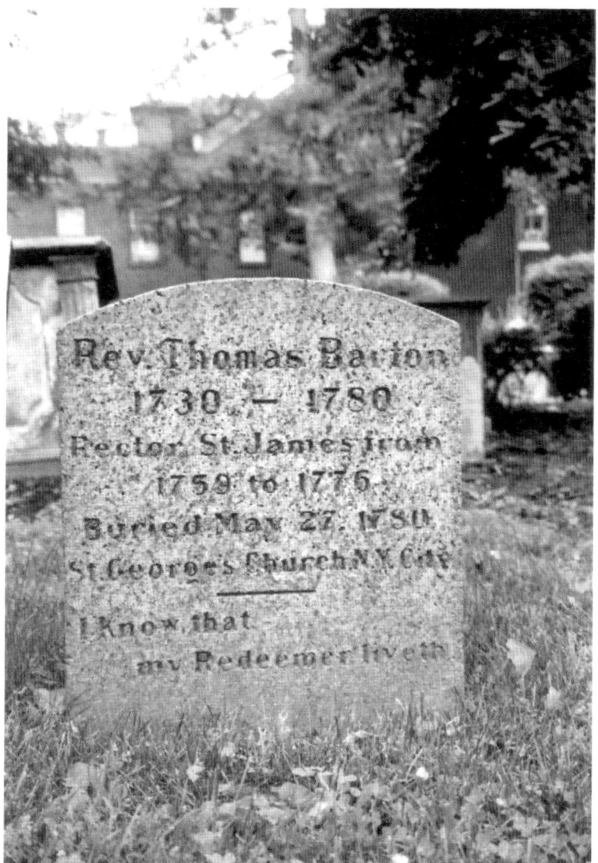

The Reverend Thomas Barton's memorial stone in St. James Episcopal Church cemetery. *Photo by the author.*

Next to their tombstones, the church has erected small historical plaques. Barton's plaque does not refer to the Conestoga incident. Shippen's plaque lists several of his life achievements and incorrectly notes that he was "Chief Burgess of Lancaster at time of Paxton Massacre."

While the graves of the Conestogas are unmarked, memorials to the two men whose names fill the third and fourth blank spaces at the beginning of this chapter are highly visible. Shippen and Barton are a focus of cemetery tours. In addition, Shippen has had a street and a school named for him. Barton's defection from Revolutionary Patriots is not viewed as a large liability at this late date, and Shippen's reputation has not suffered because his granddaughter married Benedict Arnold. The minister and magistrate who may have helped set up the killing of the Conestogas, and who definitely defended the killers in print and prevented their arrest and trial, are revered as leaders of eighteenth-century Lancaster.

PART 4

Death and Reconciliation

CHAPTER 14

"The Remains of the Victims of a Terrible Crime"

On the evening of January 25, 1882, Lancaster County's Moravians attended a religiously inspired diversion in the ornately designed Fulton Opera House on Prince Street. Teachers and pupils from the Lancaster Moravian Church Sunday school presented vocal and instrumental music, recitations and tableaux. The tableaux, representing events in Moravian history and other religious and rural themes, were the main attraction.

Only one of the ten tableaux related directly to local history. It was called "Massacre of Indians in the Jail Yard at Lancaster, December 27, 1763." The *Lancaster Intelligencer* described the scene: "The tableau was composed of eight or ten Paxton boys and fourteen or fifteen Indians, the former being armed with guns, pistols, knives, &c. Some of the Indians were represented as lying dead and others in attitudes of supplication or terror. This tableau had the advantage of being presented on the very spot on which the massacre took place, the opera house, occupying the site of the old jail."[45]

Theatergoers more than likely left this "Moravian Entertainment" with one of the gentler tableaux in mind—the "Spinning Scene in a Moravian Sisters' House," perhaps, or "Coming Through the Rye." Fulton audiences always have known about the Indian massacre that took place beneath their seats, but it is not necessarily what they want to think about when they are being entertained.[46]

The Fulton has been Lancaster's cultural center for more than a century and a half. Listed on the National Register of Historic Places, it was restored to its early grandeur in the 1990s. Its full-size, above-the-marquee figure of

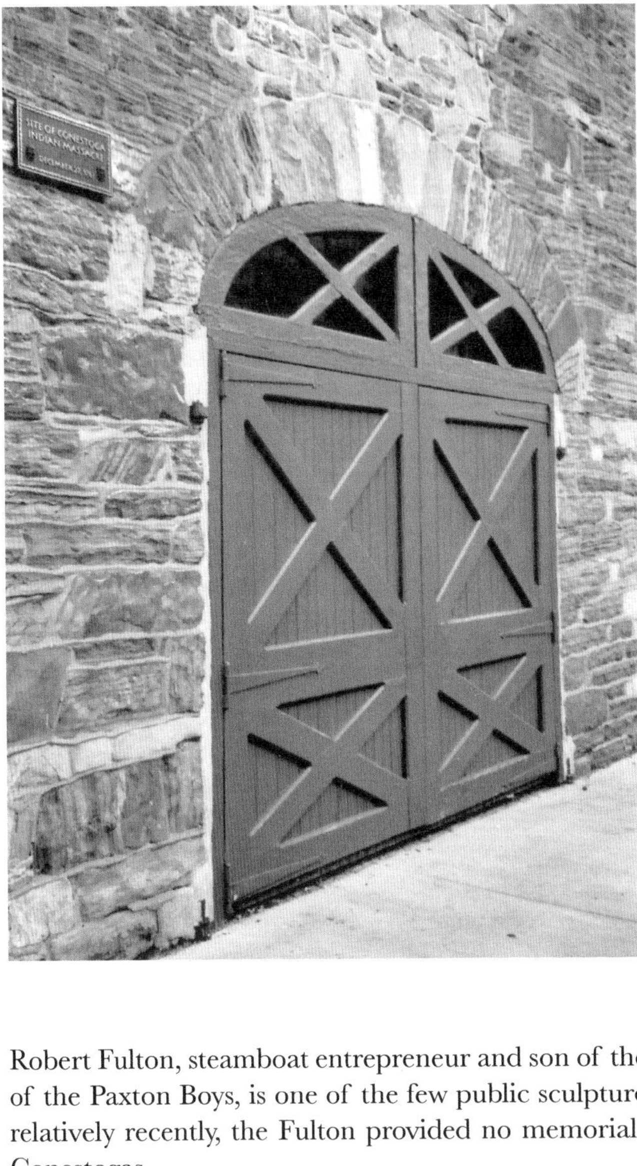

The rear wall of Lancaster's Fulton Opera House stands on the site of the massacre of the Conestoga Indians. The plaque to the left of the doors commemorates the event. *Photo by the author.*

Robert Fulton, steamboat entrepreneur and son of the Scots-Irish supporter of the Paxton Boys, is one of the few public sculptures in the city. But until relatively recently, the Fulton provided no memorial to the murder of the Conestogas.

In the summer of 1997, workmen embedded a black iron plaque near the large doors in the Fulton's stone wall on Water Street. Its gold embossing simply states, "Site of Conestoga Indian Massacre—December 27, 1763." A more detailed companion piece inside the theater reads, in part, "They were not guilty of any crime other than being at this place during that turbulent time."

Hundreds of American Indians and other Lancastrians who believed the Conestogas deserved belated respect and recognition gathered at the rear of the Fulton to dedicate the plaques and to honor the dead Conestogas on June 22, 1997. Indians of several tribes wore feathers and braided sweet grass. They beat drums, danced, recited poems and sang a song, "So Long, My Noble Red Man." Burning cedar and pungent sage wafted along Water Street as dancers and singers memorialized the dead.

"This is not a day of forgiveness, but a day of healing," observed Wayne Cave, of Chambersburg. Cave and his brother, Jim Roach, beat ceremonial drums and sang Sioux songs. "These people did not die for nothing," Cave told a newspaper reporter. "It took over one hundred years for us to come together so that we can make sure this never happens to a people again."

Some members of the audience later claimed that more than cedar fumes blew down Water Street that day. Larry Trump, a resident of Elizabethtown whose great-great-grandfather was Cherokee, says he felt a wind suddenly rise and, just as suddenly, subside during the ritual.

Barry Kornhauser, the Fulton's playwright in residence, says he didn't feel a wind on the street but did experience a remarkable phenomenon inside the theater the next day. Immediately following the Sunday afternoon ritual, he had placed some sweet grass on his oversized and cluttered desk. "When I came in Monday morning, my desk was clear," he recalls. "Everything on it was scattered all over the room. I just assumed someone had come into the place searching for something and vandalized

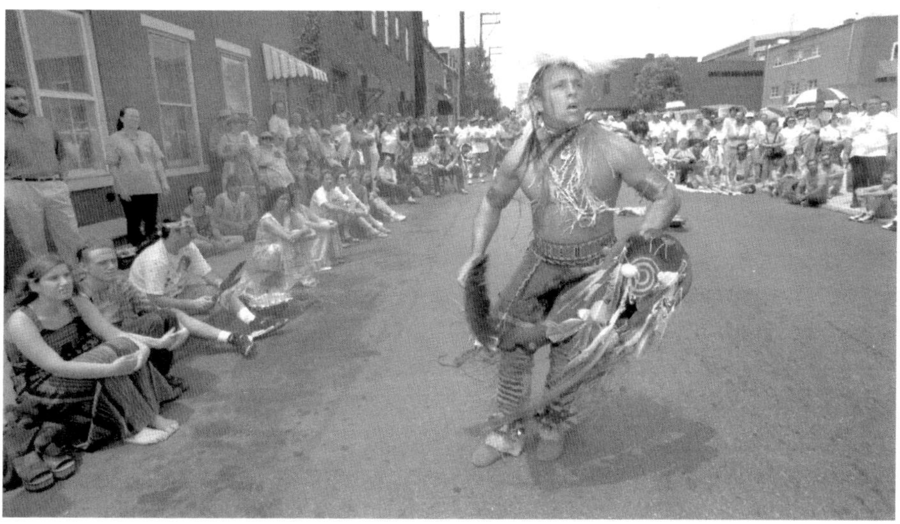

Lancaster County resident Terry Lee dances on Lancaster's Water Street during the 1997 ceremony commemorating the massacre. *Lancaster Newspapers photo by Suzette Wenger.*

the office. It wasn't until later I noticed the only thing left on the desk was the sweet grass."

A Native American later told Kornhauser that spirits manifest themselves as breezes. Although Kornhauser remains skeptical that a spirit-breeze removed everything but sweet grass from his desk, he can provide no other explanation.

Spirits are famous at the Fulton. The theater is a prime stop on a city ghost tour. When representatives of the International Ghost Hunters Society checked out the place, they developed photographs of dull white spots the size of bread plates: clear evidence, the ghost hunters said, of a paranormal presence. More literal observers have seen a woman in white, purported to be the ghost of early twentieth-century actress Mary Cahill, floating above the stage.

Some people believe ghosts of the dead Conestogas haunt the Fulton. Larry Trump and a group of Indians called Four Arrows say they have spotted ghosts in the Fulton's green room. While waiting to perform, the group saw a strange light on the wall facing Water Street. The grainy image they photographed looks vaguely human. The shape has an even hazier area above its "head." Trump is certain it's the ghost of a Conestoga. He says Indian ghosts are always present in the theater.

Trump claims his group represents "the first Indians in over two hundred years to get out of that place alive." In fact, the dead Conestogas left the area quickly in 1763. Jailor Donnally and a work crew dumped their bodies into a common grave in the paupers section of Nissly's, a Mennonite cemetery on Cherry Alley, several blocks northeast of the workhouse. For many years, an earthen mound marked the spot, near the corner of Duke and Chestnut Streets.

In the spring of 1833, workmen cutting the Pennsylvania Railroad through Lancaster disinterred these bones. Lancaster historian John W.W. Loose believes the laborers hauled many of the bones, along with other fill, out to the railroad embankment in the rear of Lancaster's McCaskey High School. Others say the bones were reburied south of Lancaster, possibly along the Conestoga River.

In any event, the railroad workers put some of the bones they uncovered while building the railroad cut into a large packing case and reburied it nearby on land eventually purchased by William Gorrecht. In the summer of 1876, Gorrecht was digging foundation trenches for a stable behind his house at 221 North Cherry Street when he exhumed this big box of bones. He gave one of the skulls he found to a local tribe of the Improved Order of Red Men, a fraternity of white men dedicated to venerating the Indians then being destroyed in the American West. He reburied the rest of the bones in the box.

At some point, the railroad constructed a concrete retaining wall along the south side of the railroad cut to keep buildings from collapsing into the ditch. In the spring of 1889, while workmen were rebuilding this wall, which had been weakened by the caving in of the embankment on Gorrecht's property, they struck the old bone box with their picks. "The wood was rotten," reported a local newspaper at the time, "and the bones rolled out. There were eight skulls and a pile of other bones, all well-preserved, the earth in that neighborhood being possessed of a peculiar quality, which keeps the bones intact." A crowd gathered to examine "the remains of the victims of a terrible crime." Then the wall builders buried the bones for a fourth time.

Since 1889, the remains of the Conestogas apparently have remained underground, although at least one person had plans to unearth them again. Ann Rongione lived at 221 North Cherry Street, in a house on Gorrecht's former property. She told a reporter that when she was a young girl, about the time the railroad filled in the cut in the late 1920s, someone wanted to dig for Indian bones in the family's backyard. Mrs. Rongione said her mother abruptly dismissed the digger.

To ease the girl's mind, Mrs. Rongione's mother told her, "Now, don't worry about it. They had to be buried somewhere. They're not going to get out and go dancing around."

CHAPTER 15

"Slaughter'd, Kill'd and Cut Off a Whole Tribe"

While the bones of the Conestogas murdered in the workhouse have been uncovered and reburied repeatedly, the graves of the Conestogas killed at Indian Town may never be discovered. No one knows the precise site of the Conestogas' final village, so it would be all but impossible to locate the six bodies that undoubtedly were buried near the burned cabins, probably in a common grave.[47]

Barry Kent, a retired state archaeologist with the Pennsylvania Historical and Museum Commission, knows more about the Susquehannocks and Conestogas than anyone. He has spent decades considering where the Conestogas lived and died on the four-hundred-acre Manor Township tract.

"My guess is that they moved around a lot over the sixty-, almost seventy-odd years that they were there," says the affable author of *Susquehanna's Indians*. "They would have worn out the village areas and they could pick things up and move them three or four thousand yards to a new location. So there are probably things scattered all around there."

In 1972, Kent found artifacts from three cabins, five small cemeteries and a half-dozen storage pits during a dig at a site just east of a hill known to local residents as Indian Round Top. The site is on the Witmer property, just north of Indian Marker Road and just west of Safe Harbor Road. It is the only large site ever excavated within the four-hundred-acre Conestoga tract.

A number of other archaeologists, professional and amateur, previously had dug up hundreds of artifacts at that place. While at least one of them was certain the last Conestoga village had been located there, Kent became

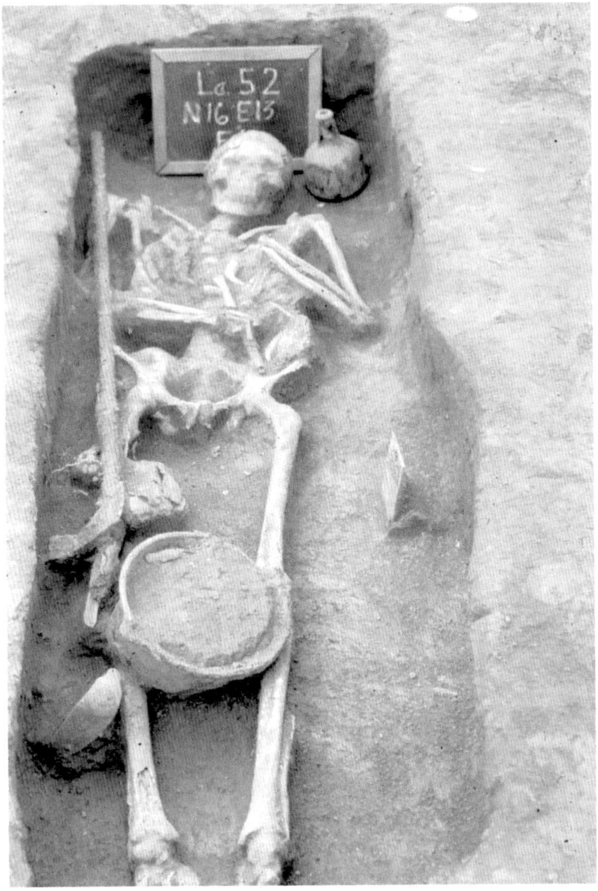

A Conestoga Indian skeleton, with personal accouterments, excavated at Conestoga Indian Town site near Indian Round Top in 1972. *State Museum of Pennsylvania, Pennsylvania Historical and Museum Commission.*

equally sure that assumption was wrong.[48] The oldest items in his excavation dated to before 1740. The Conestogas who lived until 1763, he says, would have used more recent items in the final village.

The memorial to Indian Town at the juncture of Safe Harbor and Indian Marker Roads sidesteps the issue of precisely where the Indians lived and died. It says only that the Conestogas "located their village variously on these lands in the Penn proprietary manor of Conestoga chiefly west of this point."

Determining where the Conestogas lived at any particular time is complicated by an abundance of archaeological artifacts and incomplete excavations. Farmers in the region periodically plow up projectile points, pieces of pottery, pipe stems, combs, beads and bones. Sometimes it is difficult to know whether these objects come from town sites or are simply scattered debris.

A layer of archaeological material underlies much of Manor Township. American Indian artifacts have been found at hundreds of locations, especially near the Susquehanna and Conestoga Rivers. The Conestoga Indians lived within a limited area, but their ancestors, the Susquehannocks, lived all over the region—and everywhere left behind the detritus of a once-mighty civilization.

Several thousand Susquehannocks moved here by the mid- to late sixteenth century. They settled along the Susquehanna in what would become the Washington Boro area of Manor Township, several miles northwest of the Conestoga site Kent excavated. Here they constructed a large, fortified town and other villages from which they controlled south-central Pennsylvania. In 1608, John Smith met a formidable group of Susquehannocks near the mouth of the Susquehanna and famously described them as "Giants."

By the early 1670s, however, invading Iroquois and insidious smallpox had decimated the tribe. The Susquehannocks moved across the river to York County, where the Iroquois decisively defeated them. Then they headed south, where Marylanders and Virginians killed their chiefs and dispersed their followers. The survivors returned to Pennsylvania in the 1680s and settled at Conestoga. From that time on, they were known as Conestogas.

Indian Town became a trading center for all Indians in the region. James Logan, the provincial secretary who lived primarily in Philadelphia, maintained a trading store a few miles east of the village and worked hard to maintain the exchange of Indian furs for European goods. Conestoga also became a convenient center for negotiations between various Indian groups and Pennsylvania's proprietors. Logan and a succession of governors frequently visited Conestoga. Just as often, Conestogas traveled to Philadelphia to deal directly with the proprietors.

Indian Town and its residents appear regularly in colonial records during the early decades of the eighteenth century. Some of these accounts clearly show that the proprietors and their agents paid serious attention to the 1701 treaty with William Penn. One of the articles of that treaty pledged that Penn and other English leaders would not permit "Any Act of Hostility or Violence, wrong or Injury, to or against any of the Said Indians." Until the French and Indian War, Pennsylvania rigidly honored its commitment to protect the Conestogas.

One early example: in the winter of 1722, the fur-trading brothers John and Edmond Cartlidge traveled well west of Conestoga to meet with Sawantaeny, a Seneca Indian who was trapping on a tributary of the Potomac River. After an all-night drinking session, the Cartlidges killed the Indian.

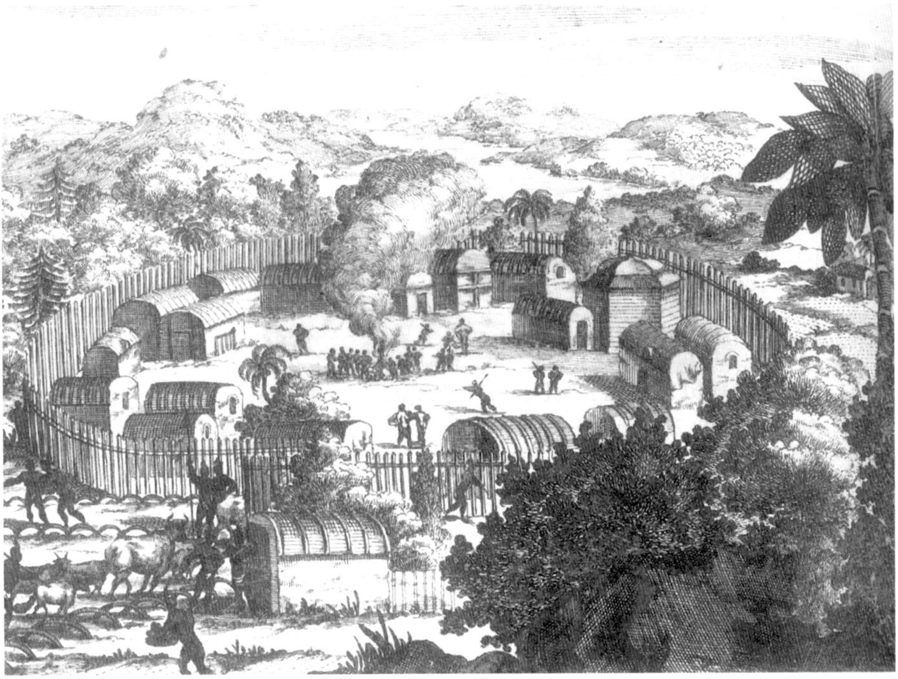

Engraving of the last Susquehannock Fort, originally published at Amsterdam in 1671. Several years later, the Iroquois captured this fort and dispersed the Susquehannocks. *John Carter Brown Library at Brown University.*

Provincial authorities told Logan to resolve the situation. He conducted an intensive investigation at Conestoga, taking depositions from witnesses and interrogating them in a courtlike setting. Then, although John Cartlidge was a prominent Lancaster County magistrate and Edmond Cartlidge the county tax collector, Logan sent them to a Philadelphia prison.

Nevertheless, while leaders on both sides continued to respect the provisions of treaties and made an effort to ensure that justice for Europeans and Indians did not differ, the Conestogas found themselves in an increasingly inferior economic and political position as the century progressed. By 1740, the possible end date for the Conestoga village Kent excavated, heavy hunting and trapping had depleted fur-bearing animals in Manor Township, and many traders had moved west of the Susquehanna where bear and beaver remained plentiful. The Conestogas could hardly hunt in forests denuded of animal life, but their neighbors' hogs and cattle regularly rooted through Indian gardens for food. The great treaty meeting of 1744, the most important of the colonial era, was held not at Conestoga but at Lancaster, signaling a change in status for the old Indian village. Supposedly some of the "principal men" of Conestoga attended the sessions, but no one recorded their names.

The Indians became increasingly dependent on their neighbors and the government. By the 1750s, many observers viewed the Conestogas as a pathetic remnant of the Susquehannock nation. The Indians were "clustered together in miserable huts," wrote the Lancaster historian Alexander Harris in 1872, "and were in the habit of gathering a pitiable subsistence by beggary and a petty merchandizing amongst the white settlers of the country around them. The men spent most of their time in fishing and hunting, and loitering around in idleness. In their neighborhood they passed for innocent vagabonds."

The Indians had a low view of themselves. At a conference with the Indian interpreter Conrad Weiser in 1750, a Conestoga declared: "Many of our old people are dead, so that we are now left as it were Orphans in a destitute condition, which inclines us to leave our old Habitations."

Even as the tribe declined, Pennsylvania officials continued to court the Conestogas as government wards and opposed their near-annual threats to leave their "old Habitations" and move north where hunting boundaries would be less rigid. If the Paxton Rangers had not intervened in December 1763, the Conestogas no doubt would have talked about migrating in the spring of 1764.

In the early 1760s, two Indians at Conestoga, advancing in years, evidently decided they would become a burden if the tribe did migrate. So they left Indian Town and sought protection from Christian Hershey, a Mennonite farmer and ancestor of Milton Hershey, founder of the chocolate company. These Conestogas, known only as Michael and Mary, were living on the Hershey farm near the small Lancaster County town of Manheim when the Paxton Rangers swept into Conestoga and Lancaster and wiped out the rest of the tribe. According to family tradition, the Indians hid in the basement of the Hershey home until the fever for Indian killing had passed.

In the summer of 1764, John Penn provided a certificate for Michael and Mary's protection. This certificate required all persons "to suffer them to pass and re-pass on their lawful business without the least molestation or interruption." Three years later, visiting Moravian missionary Bernhard Adam Grube found Michael away from home. But he described Mary as "happy as a child."

The couple lived well into their eighties in a hut beside a little stream in a meadow near the Hershey residence. Today small fieldstones mark their graves. Dairyman Noah Kreider Jr., whose mother was a Hershey, recalls being impressed by the grave site as a young boy. "I wanted to dig here, just to see what

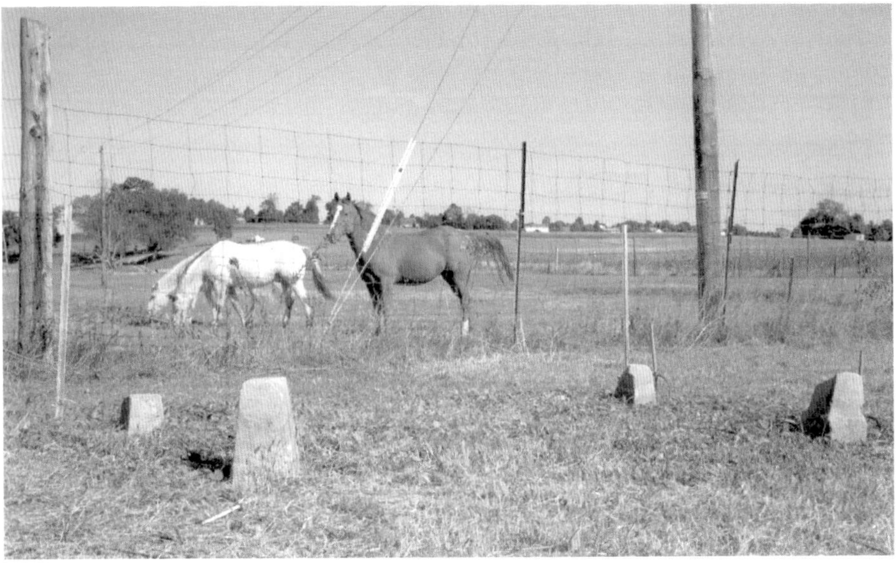

Head and foot stones mark graves of the last of the Conestogas, Michael and Mary, on a farm outside Manheim, Lancaster County. *Photo by the author.*

I could find," he says. Kreider never disturbed the graves, but he did uncover projectile points, probably used by previous occupants, throughout the meadow.

Some believe that Michael and Mary, who had no children, were the last of the Conestoga tribe. But there are other traditions. In northeastern Lancaster County, people say that another Conestoga who escaped both massacres was secreted on a Brecknock Township farm for the rest of his life.

Others say there were several survivors who have many descendants. Because the Conestogas and Senecas intermingled, there are living Senecas who claim Conestoga or Susquehannock blood. Barry Kent is not impressed by these claims. "Some of the similar genetics is still floating around, probably on the Seneca reservations," he concedes, "but you couldn't prove any of it—and so what?" Short of matching DNA somehow uncovered from a grave site, Kent says, there is no way to know whether someone is a Susquehannock or Conestoga descendant. "There couldn't be any genealogical research to say, 'I'm a Susquehannock,' because the records weren't kept," he concludes. "The oral traditions are, I think, largely fabrications."

In any case, the Conestogas, as a tribe, did abruptly cease to exist in 1763. They were among the early casualties of what would become the U.S. government's official policy of dispossessing Indians of their land by removing or killing them.

CHAPTER 16

"Who Was Left to Mourn for These People?"

On September 13, 1924, one thousand spectators gathered to observe the unveiling of the memorial boulder to the Conestogas. The rugged rock had been hauled out of the ravine that the Paxton Rangers had followed east from the Susquehanna and had been rooted again several miles to the east near Indian Town. A bronze plaque bolted to the boulder informed observers that the Conestogas had resided in this vicinity until they were "exterminated by the Paxton Boys in 1763."

David Herr Landis, a local archaeologist and historian who had done considerable excavating in the area, chaired the event and presented the main address. He spoke at length about the history of the Susquehannocks, reminding his listeners that "this was then a veritable Indian paradise," before describing the massacre. Landis paused at one point in his talk to marvel at the senselessness of what had occurred. "It seems incredible," he told the assembly, "that after years of poverty and struggle the last remnant of this once noble tribe was murdered by Europeans."

That result probably did not seem so incredible to the final speaker of the day. Chief Joseph Strong Wolf, an Ojibway from northern Wisconsin, wore native regalia and carried a red ceremonial pipe. The *Papers* of the Lancaster County Historical Society described him as "a splendid type of the Red Man of today...a full blooded relative of the extinct tribe of the Conestogas."

Strong Wolf wanted the assembly to understand that he had returned from France "thoroughly disgusted with the barbarity of the white man." He had been wounded twice in the world war, he said, and yet remained ineligible

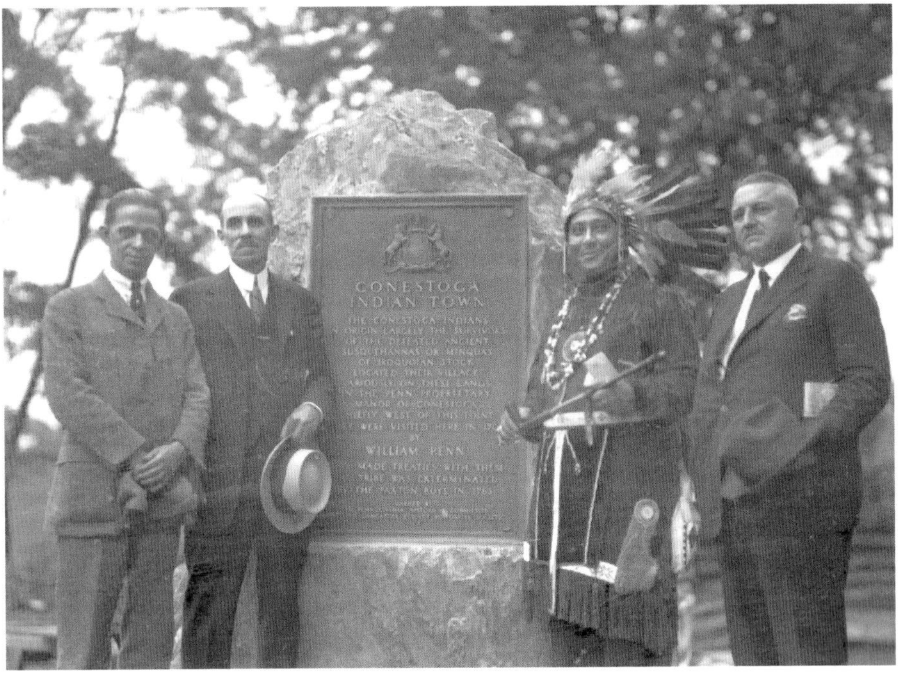

Dignitaries attend the dedication of a boulder memorializing the Conestogas near Indian Town in 1924. David H. Landis, an archaeologist who chaired the event, stands immediately left of the boulder. Chief Joseph Strong Wolf, an Ojibway Indian from Wisconsin, stands at right. *Lancaster Newspapers.*

to vote in the country he had served. But Strong Wolf commended the way Quakers had treated the Conestogas in Pennsylvania, "the only bright spot in the otherwise dark page of the record of the White man's dealing with the Red." He also praised the historical and archaeological studies of David Landis, without whom the Conestogas would "lie in oblivion."

An earlier speaker, Herbert H. Beck, president of the county's historical society, had tried to explain why the Conestogas had been all but forgotten. "The displacement of the Indian in America," he informed the assembled crowd, "is only one episode recurrent in history—the establishment of an expansive, better informed people." Thus did the local historian, parroting Francis Parkman and apparently oblivious to the sensibilities of the college-educated Strong Wolf, describe Indian "displacement" to his "better informed" listeners.

A widespread belief that the demise of Indian civilization was an inevitable side effect of European colonization continued well into the twentieth century.

In "The Historic Role of the Susquehannocks" in *Susquehannock Miscellany* (1959), William Hunter, the Pennsylvania Historical and Museum Commission researcher who later revealed Redmond Conyngham's fabricated "Provincial Correspondence," bluntly argued that "the historian must almost necessarily relate the history of an Indian group—or that of the Indians in general—to the main stream of American history, which is western European in origin and affiliation. This point has been expressed somewhat harshly by asserting that Indian history does not exist, that the Indian is in practical fact an incident of white history."

Ethnocentric historians and archaeologists have had to make way in recent decades for a fresh perspective. As Daniel Richter noted in *Facing East from Indian Country*, published just inside the twenty-first century: "A story line that follows only the exploits of the English-speaking few strips the past of much of its real drama, its explanatory power, and—increasingly in a century when people of European descent are again expected to become a minority in North America—its relevance for the present."

The academic perspective is changing.

But if a greater appreciation for American Indian history is to advance significantly, that change will have to come not only through academic reevaluations but also through a humanistic reappraisal of what it meant and means to be a Native American in a country that annihilated most of its Indians. That is especially true in Pennsylvania, where there are no reservations and relatively few Indians among the general population and the state government recognizes no Indian tribes.

In Lancaster County, that reappraisal has begun among the Anabaptists.

During the Reformation in sixteenth- and seventeenth-century Switzerland, a religious group decided that baptism should be reserved for adults who understood the meaning of their commitment to the church. When these Anabaptists refused to baptize infants, Swiss Reformed Church ministers reviled and persecuted them; they drowned and beheaded them; they boiled them in oil.

Thousands of Anabaptists fled to America. Many settled in Lancaster County, where they formed Mennonite, Amish and Brethren congregations.

In 2003, Swiss Reformed ministers, seeking forgiveness for their predecessors' persecution, invited Lancaster's Anabaptists to return to Switzerland, where they began a process of reconciliation. Two years later, these ministers traveled to Lancaster County and held a similar session.

Meanwhile, a number of progressive Anabaptists began a parallel process, seeking forgiveness for persecuting Native Americans. In October 2003—240 years after the Conestoga massacre—a group of Lancaster Mennonites and evangelicals met with representatives of the Iroquois. Janet Keller Richards, author of a book on reconciliation, helped assemble the Mennonites and other interested Lancastrians. They took the Iroquois on a tour of sites connected with the Conestogas. The Lancastrians asked for forgiveness for their ancestors' sins of killing the Indians and stealing their land.

Oneida leader Ivan Doxtator, of First Nations Counseling Ministries, and Mohawk pastor Willie Jock represented the Iroquois. While visiting Turkey Hill along the Susquehanna River, just west of the first massacre site, Doxtator talked of the "deep pain" he felt. "There was a tremendous sense of grief there in identifying with [the dead Conestogas]," he said.

Then the group visited Lancaster's Penn Square, where the Paxton Rangers had stabled their horses at Matthias Slough's tavern while they killed the Conestogas and later had ridden around the county courthouse in celebration. After a reading of the names of the dead Indians, Doxtator asked, "Who was left to mourn for these people?" He quickly answered, "There was no one left." And then he lamented that the Rangers had killed Will Sock and other Conestogas even though they had become Christians.

The Anabaptists again asked for forgiveness because the Paxton Rangers were never punished by the county's magistrates. And they said the Conestogas' Anabaptist neighbors shared the guilt for that injustice because, as "the quiet in the land," they did nothing to promote justice. The Iroquois agreed that neither the church nor the justice system had helped the Conestogas, but they forgave both ministers and magistrates. Then the Anabaptists and the Iroquois embraced, completing the reconciliation process.

In October 2010, as part of the celebration of the tercentennial of the first Lancaster County Mennonite settlement, the Lancaster Mennonite Historical Society sponsored a meeting to expand on the reconciliation theme. Representatives of Mennonite, Quaker and Presbyterian churches acknowledged to several Indian groups that early Pennsylvanians were wrong to break treaties and massacre the Conestogas.

Significantly, this meeting was held at Edward Shippen's primary church, First Presbyterian, in Lancaster. It was the first time that Presbyterians had acknowledged their church's role in the massacre. The Presbyterians criticized John Elder for not doing more to stop the Paxton Rangers. They asked that "our native brothers and sisters forgive the wrongs done to them so long ago." In place of the biblical verse cited as justification for killing

Indians in 1763, the Presbyterians quoted from 2 Chronicles 7:14, which pledges that if people repent, God "will forgive their sin and heal their land."[49]

During preparations for this reconciliation, Mennonite representative Lloyd Hoover said, "We, as Europeans, basically annihilated the Susquehannocks who were here, and to the rest of the tribes we committed acts that scattered them across the nation. Any way that I connect to that as a European and a Mennonite and a Christian, I ask for forgiveness." Apache representative Gray Wolf responded, "If our forefathers heard what we were talking about here, they'd be dancing with joy."

Perhaps. The past is not so easy to neutralize. The "blot on the history of Lancaster county which no one can ever remove," as a local historian characterized the massacre in 1914, remains indelible even as some members of the community finally acknowledge and apologize for the actions of their ancestors.

Many Lancastrians still know little or nothing about what happened in 1763. Except for the memorial boulder at Safe Harbor and Indian Marker Roads, another historical marker at Safe Harbor itself and the plaque at the rear doors of the Fulton Opera House, there are no visible signs that the area remembers its darkest moment.

A quarter of a millennium has passed.

Even as steady growth has swelled Lancaster's population past half a million, the county remains nationally recognized for its agricultural production and farmland preservation. Thanks to a diversified economy based largely on agriculture, varied business and industry and tourism, most county residents enjoy a comfortable standard of living, even during an extended recession. Dozens of retirement communities have propelled Lancaster onto *Forbes* magazine's list of the top ten places to grow old.

Lancaster attracts throngs of tourists who ogle the gently rolling farm fields and the horse-and-buggy Amish, the scenic stone mills and covered bridges in the country and the fashionable brick townhouses in the city. The visitors gorge on egg noodles and soft pretzels, shop in some of the nation's largest outlet malls and drop their jaws at expansive productions in music and religious theaters. Many like what they see and come back to stay; but the county's base remains solidly home-grown, Caucasian, Republican and Christian.

Lancaster is known as the Garden Spot of Pennsylvania, the northernmost link in the nation's Bible Belt and "a perfect place to settle down and raise a family."

By those who care about how Lancaster came to be, the county also is known as the place that, during the harsh December of 1763, killed all of its Indians.

The Bodies of the Murdered were then brought out and exposed in the Street, till a Hole could be made in the Earth, to receive and cover them. But the Wickedness cannot be covered, the Guilt will lie on the whole Land, till Justice is done on the Murderers. THE BLOOD OF THE INNOCENT WILL CRY TO HEAVEN FOR VENGEANCE.

—*Benjamin Franklin,* A Narrative of the Late Massacres, in Lancaster County, of a Number of Indians, Friends of this Province, By Persons Unknown. With some Observations on the same, *1764*

"Why didn't the Indians kill all the white people?"
"They didn't have the heart for it."
"But didn't white people kill most of the Indians?"
"Yes, they did."

—*Sherman Alexie, dialogue from* Indian Killer, *1996*

Notes

1. "Drive the Heathen Out of the Land"

1. Paxton and Derry townships were part of Lancaster County until the creation of Dauphin County in 1785. Harris's Ferry eventually became Harrisburg, Dauphin County. Donegal Township remains in Lancaster County.
2. Wright's Ferry became Columbia, Lancaster County.

2. "Some Hot Headed Ill Advised Persons"

3. Prison Run, later called Roaring Brook, is no longer visible. Its water flows through a huge pipe buried beneath present-day Water Street.

3. "The Same Spirit & Frantic Rage"

4. The term "Paxton Boys" was first used, in a disparaging way, in a political pamphlet in April 1764. Paxton Boys eventually became the generic name for any group of vigilantes looking for a fight.
5. This bill eventually passed. Benjamin Franklin and his Quaker friends argued successfully that if the killers were identified and charged, they could not receive a fair hearing in Lancaster County, where a jury sympathetic to men long oppressed by hostile Indians probably would acquit them. But the law was never carried out. Opponents of the bill argued that English common law stipulated that a trial be held in the county where the crime was committed.

6. The scalp bounty expired in December 1764 when John Penn proclaimed an end to hostilities. Historian Henry Young could find no evidence that any reward was paid or even claimed.

4. "Persons of Undoubted Probity & Veracity"

7. The undated manuscript of the *Apology*, a diatribe against Indians and Quakers housed at the Historical Society of Pennsylvania, was written in ink on nineteen pages of a small leather-bound book. It is obviously a draft, with numerous words crossed out or added. The affidavits themselves—inserted, without explanation, into the middle of the text—appear to have been copied in ink from another source because only one minor error has been corrected. Both the *Apology* and its affidavits appear to have been written by the same hand.
8. According to a direct descendant, Alexander Stephens was known as a "rough man" who may have been "fraternizing with the enemy." Owen Stephens, of Washington, Georgia, explains, "It stands to reason that the Indians communicated to him as one they trusted quite well. Else, if he were foe, they'd not reveal such incriminating facts."
9. The anonymous writer of a 1764 pamphlet (*An Answer to the Pamphlet Entitled "The Conduct of the Paxton-Men"*) thought the affidavits "were all trumpet up, since the Indians were Murdered, to gloss over that horrid act. Was the like ever known before? For a set of Men, in Conspiracy together, to fall upon and Murder a number of their Neighbors, and then ransack the Earth, to find Evidence to prove that they were dangerous Neighbours; and that they had received but their deserts. This is a very odd Affair, first to kill a Man, then to pass Sentence on him, and after all that to produce the Evidence against him."
10. These unsubstantiated charges impressed some people. John Ewing, a prominent Presbyterian pastor in Philadelphia, provost of the University of Pennsylvania and father-in-law of John Harris's daughter, found them sound and expanded them in a February 1764 letter to Joseph Reed, a Scots-Irishman then in England. Ewing was convinced that the Conestogas "entertained the French and Indian spies—gave intelligence to them of the defenseless state of our Province—furnished them with our Gazette every week, or fortnight—gave them intelligence of all the dispositions of the Province army against them…—actually murdered and scalped some of the Frontier inhabitants—insolently boasted of the murders they had committed…confessed that they had been at war with us, and would soon be at war with us again." These things and more, Ewing claimed, had been "proved upon oath."

5. "I Never Heard One Word of It Till It Was Just Over"

11. "Young Joe Hays" is almost certainly a reference to Ess-canesh, the son of Sohays, or Sheehays, the oldest of the Conestogas. However, Shippen must have confused Ess-canesch with Tong-quas, or Chrisly, the boy who escaped the massacre and fled to Thomas McKee's farm. Ess-canesch died with his father at Conestoga.

6. "A Mighty Noise and Hubbub"

12. The public debate by pamphlet was accompanied by a private debate by letter. John Ewing, the Scots-Irish pastor of First Presbyterian Church in Philadelphia, told John Reed in February 1764 that "few, but Quakers, think that the Lancaster Indians have suffered any thing but their just deserts. 'Tis not a little surprising to us here, that orders should be sent from the Crown, to apprehend and bring to justice those persons who have cut off that nest of enemies that lived near Lancaster." Contrarily, *Hazard's Register* reported in 1833 that an anonymous Quaker had written to an "Old Friend" in February 1764 that the "heroes" who had killed the Conestogas were engaged in a "holy war" in which "neither the mother nor the tender infant that hung at the breast, was spared, though on her knees she begged for mercy."
13. Franklin could not have known such intimate details about individual Conestogas unless someone familiar with the Indians had informed him. His most likely source was Susanna Wright, daughter of the ferry master at Wright's Ferry. She knew the Indians well and frequently corresponded with Franklin on a variety of subjects.
14. This appears to be a reference to Susanna Wright, Franklin's friend in Wright's Ferry.

7. "Shot—Scalped—Hacked—and Cut to Pieces"

15. Thomas Pynchon expanded on Mason's observations in his 1997 novel, *Mason & Dixon*. Following a tour of the workhouse, where he observes "blood in Corners never cleans'd," Pynchon's Dixon exclaims, "What in the Holy Names are these people about? Not even the Dutchmen at the Cape behaved this way. Is it something in this Wilderness, something ancient, that waited for them, and infected their Souls when they came?"
16. Similarly, Susanna Wright, of Wright's Ferry, briefly described the massacre in terms of personal experience with the Indians in a paragraph

published in Watson's *Annals of Philadelphia* nearly half a century after her death: "The cruel murder of these poor Indians has affected and discomposed my mind beyond what I can express. We had known the greater part of them from children; had been always intimate with them. Three or four of the women were sensible and civilized, and the Indians' children used to play with ours and oblige them all they could."

17. This Christie is no doubt the Chrisly named and so spelled by Sheriff John Hay in his list of the twenty Conestogas killed at Conestoga and Lancaster.

8. "One of Those Youthful Ebullitions of Wrath"

18. James Hamilton, a Philadelphia businessman, immediately preceded John Penn as the colony's chief executive. He also owned and laid out the lots of Lancaster in the 1730s.

19. Watson's *Annals of Philadelphia* reported in 1857 that Thomas Elder, one of John Elder's sons and a Harrisburg attorney, claimed that the minister "rode after the Paxton boys, and got at their head to turn them back, and they declared they would shoot him down." That the Rangers would have threatened to kill their commander and minister seems unlikely. Watson also said the party took sacrament at Paxton Presbyterian before heading toward the Conestogas' village. This seems less unlikely.

20. The ages of the children, however, can be questioned. In his *Narrative*, Franklin said the dead included "children of a Year old." But Reaves Goehring, a retired Columbia High School history teacher, speculates that most of the children were not babies who demanded constant parental attention but "of elementary school age," who required less care. Therefore, their young parents could serve as spies or even active warriors in Pontiac's Rebellion. "Where were the parents during the massacre?" Goehring asks. "They were out on the frontier. Out on the warpath, little tiny kids would be more of a hindrance than anything else. But if grandpa and grandma can babysit, why you're free to come and go a little."

21. This is another product of Redmond Conyngham's imagination. According to Leo Shelley, St. James's historian, the church's original bell was not hung in the steeple until 1771.

22. Redmond Conyngham cited six affidavits in his 1843 series in the *Intelligencer.* They were not the same six as listed in the *Apology of the Paxton Volunteers* but a selection of some of the affidavits the Reverend Thomas Barton had printed in "The Conduct of the Paxton-Men." Before offering his specimens, Conyngham claimed there were "many more."

9. "THE INNOCENT WERE DESTINED TO SHARE THE FATE OF THE GUILTY"

23. In 1953, Conrad Richter had dramatized the Rangers' hatred for Indians in *The Light in the Forest*, the slim novel that remains the introductory reading on the massacre for many young Pennsylvanians. True Son, who was captured by Indians as a young child and grew up to embrace them as a teenager, hears one account of the Conestoga massacre from his blood uncle, a Ranger: "They got what they deserved. We fixed the men so they wouldn't butcher any more of our people. And we fixed the squaws and young ones so they wouldn't breed any more murderers." True Son's Indian "father" also tells of the massacre: "The white barbarians scalped them. They did indecencies. They chopped off the hands of the men and squaws. They put guns in the mouth of one of our Conestogo cousins while he was yet speaking and blew his head to pieces."
24. The idea that the Paxton "riots" were primarily political in nature has become a flashpoint for controversy. For example, three years after Jacobs's book appeared, James E. Crowley proposed in an article in *Pennsylvania History* that the divisions between the frontiersmen and the government, the backcountry and Philadelphia were more societal than political: "The Paxtonians had a more simplistic conception of the composition of society and did not feel that order was important except as it involved their peace and security."

10. "A ZONE OF VICIOUS RACIAL VIOLENCE"

25. Charles Hanna was more pointed in his remarks about "lynching" in *The Scotch-Irish or The Scot in North Britain, North Ireland, and North America* (1902): "(The Conestoga massacre) is said by some to have been the first instance of the operation of lynch law in America; and many blame the Scotch-Irish for its introduction. Doubtless the odium is merited."

11. "THE MOST RESPECTABLE OF MEN"

26. Some men who rode with the Paxton Rangers undoubtedly were drawn as well from Derry Presbyterian Church, the nearby congregation that John Elder also served. Early chroniclers of the massacres, including Benjamin Franklin, Robert Proud and I. Daniel Rupp, reported that some of the killers also came from Donegal, meaning the township and Donegal Presbyterian Church. Historian George Franz believes they were correct. But Donegal-area historian Mary Karnes reports that she has "never read of any such admission. Perhaps they all just succeeded in remaining incognito."

27. Elder's home, at Twenty-second and Ellerslie Streets, is the oldest building still standing in the city of Harrisburg. Isolated by several acres of lawn from row homes in its modest neighborhood, the house has never left the Elder family.
28. "Stranger Indians" or simply "strange Indians" is a term commonly used in colonial writing. "Strange Indians" were any Indians that a white observer did not know. Often they were suspected of being hostile Indians or spies for hostiles.
29. Although often identified by historians as a "colonel," Elder was not commissioned. John Penn directed Elder to act as a "commander," that is as a recruiter and organizer of militia.
30. Practically every historian who has written about the Conestoga massacre since 1843 has called Lazarus Stewart the leader of the Paxton Rangers. Outside Redmond Conyngham's fabrication in the *Lancaster Intelligencer & Journal*, however, the only allegation targeting Stewart in any way is J.P. De Haas's deposition of 1770, and it does not identify him as the Rangers' leader.

12. "They Had Possession and Would Keep It"

31. Soldiers in the regular and provincial armies shared the Paxton militia's attitude. They began losing interest in making a distinction between hostile and neutral Indians during the French and Indian War. This disinterest was advanced by Pontiac's Rebellion. Peter Silver explains in *Our Savage Neighbors* that some army officers in 1763 freely discussed killing all Indians, regardless of affiliation, by any means possible.
32. Daniel Richter (*Facing East from Indian Country*) notes that racist attitudes ran both ways: "During the Revolutionary era, ethnic cleansing was a powerful urge on both sides of a newly deepening racial divide…There were, then, at least two wars for independence—one Indian and one White. And both traced their origins to 1763. Not coincidentally, the same year saw two parallel campaigns of ethnic cleansing, one proclaimed by the Ottawa war chief Pontiac, the other by the Pennsylvania vigilantes known as the 'Paxton Boys.'"
33. Just before the Conestogas were killed, a group of merchants from Lancaster and Philadelphia who had suffered losses to hostile Indians in the French and Indian War gathered in Philadelphia to claim compensation from the government. If they could not get that, they said, they wanted Indian lands. Sir William Johnson said he would do his best for them when he next renegotiated the boundary line, which he did, with stunning success, at the Treaty of Fort Stanwix in New York five years later.

34. An exception, the Proclamation of 1763, forbade colonists from settling west of the Appalachian Mountains. British officials had determined that this boundary line would preserve friendly relations with the Indians and contribute to the security of the colonies. News of the proclamation reached Philadelphia by December 8, 1763, and Lancaster shortly thereafter. It is not known whether the Paxton Rangers, who were just days away from killing the Conestogas, had heard about the document. It is clear that the Proclamation rapidly enraged many colonists against royal authority and the Indians the proclamation sought to protect.

35. The people of Paxton had to get in line. On February 9, 1764, Sir William Johnson told John Penn that he had made a "just representation of the Massacre of the Conestoga Indians" to the Iroquois. In return, he heard the Iroquois propose that, following the extinction of the Conestogas, "the Lands they possess revert to them their Relations and next heirs." But in 1768, at the Treaty of Fort Stanwix, the Iroquois gave up all interest in the land to John Penn for $300 and another unidentified sum. In 1775, the Iroquois sold the land again, believing that land ownership could not be permanent. In 1845, Indians claiming to be descendants of the Conestogas living with the Oneidas in New York filed a legal claim for monetary compensation for the land. This futile effort continued for decades.

13. "Eternal Shame & Reproach"

36. Hay simply may have had a realistic view of his authority. Challenges to the authority of sheriffs and other law officers were common in eighteenth-century Lancaster County. When a Lancaster sheriff tried to arrest John Offner on a warrant in 1788, Offner reportedly told the sheriff to inform the justice of the peace "to mind his own business and not mine, and tell the old bugger, the damned old rascal, that he may kiss my arse."

37. The authors of the *Apology of the Paxton Volunteers*, the handwritten defense of the Paxton Boys that includes a number of affidavits against the Conestogas, adopted a radically different assessment of the magistrates' responsibility. The *Apology* explained that the government had no authority to protect "these Enemies of his Majesty against the Resentments of his injured Subjects." The authors further maintained that the magistrates understood that their offices "did not authorize them to protect these Indians for they never attempted to defend them."

38. The colonial-era Shippens were on a par with the Byrds, Lees and Randolphs of Virginia and the Hutchinsons and Winthrops of Massachusetts, according to Shippen family biographer Randolph Klein. Edward Shippen was one of the most prominent members of the family.

39. Shippen seems to have had a higher opinion of slaves than of Indians. He owned three slaves, including one named Hannah. Hannah's husband was owned by a resident of Chester, about fifty miles from Lancaster. His owner permitted him to visit Hannah on occasion. Shippen observed Hannah's joy on seeing her husband arrive and her grief when he left. He reflected that "Blacks have natural affections as well as we have."

40. Barton's authorship of the pamphlet first was mentioned by Rhoda Barber, of Columbia, who had written in her 1830 journal that "an Episcopalian minister in Lancaster wrote to vindicate [the Paxtonians] bringing scripture to prove that it was right to destroy the heathen and very many were of the same opinion." Barton's great-grandson, George Maurice Abbot, librarian of the Library Company of Philadelphia, officially verified Barton's authorship in 1873. After thoroughly examining Barton's tract and life, James Myers concluded in 1994 that Barton must have authored the pamphlet because it was written in the form of a letter, which was Barton's preference; it made a patriotic appeal to an Irish readership; its prose style is similar to Barton's; and it duplicates parts of an earlier Barton tract.

41. Myers makes this bargain even clearer in a 1995 contribution to the *Pennsylvania Magazine of History & Biography*: "[Barton's] anonymous contribution to the pamphlet war ignited by the Paxton disturbances of 1763–64 brought him new rewards, the most significant being the lifetime grant of Thomas Penn's Conestoga Manor."

42. Barton also may have had a personal reason to fear hostile Indians during his time in Adams County. According to a family story related by Thomas Barton, a descendant who lives in Norristown, the minister was away one day when his wife, Esther, cut off an Indian's fingers with an ax as he tried to climb in a window of their home.

43. In November 1763, the month before the massacres, Barton relocated to a residence on the southeast corner of North Lime and East Orange Streets. He could not have moved much closer to Edward Shippen, whose imposing stone mansion stood at the northwest corner of that intersection. The two intellectuals reportedly delighted in discussing religion, astronomy, gardening and other common interests.

44. Barton wrote little about the massacre under his own name. In a report to the Society for the Propagation of the Gospel, he commended his congregation for not getting involved "in the murder of the Indians," although clearly his parishioners would not have been involved because he had summoned them to church the afternoon the Conestogas were killed. In a letter to Sir William Johnson in 1768, Barton condemned the Rangers for "the Assassination of those hapless Wretches."

14. "THE REMAINS OF THE VICTIMS OF A TERRIBLE CRIME"

45. The Fulton Opera House does occupy the site of the jail, but that simple description can be misleading. In 1775, the original jail was expanded to the north, taking over the old workhouse. So in 1763, the Conestoga Indians were killed in the workhouse, which became part of the jail in 1775, which became part of the Fulton Opera House in 1852. Those who don't understand this progression may believe the Indians were imprisoned when they were slaughtered.
46. Leslie Stainton, a Lancaster County native and author of *Ghost Walk*, a forthcoming history and memoir of the Fulton Opera House, discussed the theater's historical demons in an essay in the winter 2006 issue of *Michigan Quarterly Review*. The theater's foundation, she wrote, "shelters that part of ourselves we most despise. In the basement of the storied Fulton Opera House, we find not the consolations of the cave, but its terrors, our ghosted past."

15. "SLAUGHTER'D, KILL'D AND CUT OFF A WHOLE TRIBE"

47. Unlike the "peculiar" quality of the soil in Lancaster City that seems to have preserved Indian bones well into the nineteenth century, archaeologists say the soil in Manor Township is full of caustic fertilizers that have accelerated the rate of decomposition. In most graves, only teeth caps remain; the skeletons are gone.
48. Digging in 1948 at the same site Kent excavated, John Witthoft, also with the state Historical and Museum Commission, based his contention that this was the final site of Indian Town on one discovery: "A single burial was found within the site, and represented an adult placed in a hole scarcely a foot deep," Witthoft reported. "The careless manner of burial and its position within the village suggest that these bone fragments represent one of the Indians killed here in 1763 and hastily buried by his White neighbors."

16. "WHO WAS LEFT TO MOURN FOR THESE PEOPLE?"

49. Presbyterians attending the reconciliation meeting in 2010 represented the Presbytery of Donegal, which includes Lancaster, York and Chester Counties. Paxton Presbyterian Church is not in the Donegal region and did not participate.

Bibliography

Manuscript and Record Collections

The Apology of the Paxton Volunteers addressed to the candid & impartial World. Historical Society of Pennsylvania, Philadelphia.

Barber, Rhoda. "A History of Settlement at Wright's Ferry on Susquehanna River." Historical Society of Pennsylvania.

Elder Collection. Dauphin County Historical Society, Harrisburg, PA.

Friendly Association Papers (David Henderson letter). Haverford College Library, Haverford, PA.

Jacob Whistler affidavit. Records of the Land Office. Pennsylvania Historical and Museum Commission, Harrisburg.

Lancaster County Papers. Historical Society of Pennsylvania.

Lancaster County Quarter Sessions Court Papers. Lancaster County Historical Society, Lancaster, PA.

Landis, David. "The Indian Site at Indian Town" in *Catalogue of My Collection of Indian Curios.* Hershey Museum, Hershey, PA.

Minutes of the Provincial Council of Pennsylvania (Colonial Records). Lancaster County Historical Society.

Pennsylvania Archives. Lancaster County Historical Society.

Shippen Papers. American Philosophical Society, Philadelphia.

———. Historical Society of Pennsylvania.

Wittoft, John."The Susquehnnock and Conestoga towns of 1640–1763." Division of Archaeology. Pennsylvania Historical and Museum Commission, Harrisburg.

SELECTED SECONDARY SOURCES

Bausman, Lottie M. "Massacre of the Conestoga Indians, 1763: Incidents and Details." *Papers of the Lancaster County Historical Society* 18, no. 1 (1914): 169–85.

Calloway, Colin G. *The Scratch of a Pen: 1763 and the Transformation of North America*. New York: Oxford University Press, 2006.

Cavaioli, Frank J. "A Profile of the Paxton Boys: Murderers of the Conestoga Indians." *Journal of the Lancaster County Historical Society* 87, no. 3 (1983): 74–96.

Conyngham, Redmond. "Historical Sketches Containing Facts Not Generally Known." *Lancaster Intelligencer & Journal* (March 28–August 22, 1843).

Cummings, Hubertis M. "The Paxton Killings." *Journal of Presbyterian History* 44, no. 4 (December 1966): 219–43.

———. *Scots Breed & Susquehanna*. Pittsburgh: University of Pittsburgh Press, 1964.

Dowd, Gregory E. *War Under Heaven: Pontiac, the Indian Nations and the British Empire*. Baltimore: Johns Hopkins University Press, 2002.

Dunbar, John R., ed. *The Paxton Papers*. The Hague, Netherlands: Martinus Nijhoff, 1957.

Egle, Wm. Henry. *History of the County of Dauphin*. Philadelphia: Everts & Peck, 1883.

———. *Notes and Queries Chiefly Relating to Interior Pennsylvania*. Harrisburg, PA: Harrisburg Publishing Co., 1879–95.

Eshleman, H. Frank. *Annals of the Susquehannocks and Other Indian Tribes of Pennsylvania, 1500–1763*. 1908; reprint, Lewisburg, PA: Wennawoods, 2000.

Franz, George W. *Paxton: A Study of Community Structure and Mobility in the Colonial Pennsylvania Backcountry*. New York: Garland, 1989.

Gordon, Thomas F. *The History of Pennsylvania*. Philadelphia: Carey, Lea & Carey, 1829.

Hanna, Charles A. *The Wilderness Trail*. 1911; reprint, Lewisburg, PA: Wennawoods, 1995.

Hazard's Register of Pennsylvania 6 (1830–31), 358; 7 (1831), 113–15; 8 (1832), 113–15; 12 (1833–34), 9–13.

Heckewelder, John. *Narrative of the Mission of the United Brethren among the Delaware and Mohegan Indians from Its Commencement in the Year 1740, to the Close of the Year 1808.* 1820; reprint, Cleveland, OH: Burrows Brothers, 1907.

Hindle, Brook. "The March of the Paxton Boys." *William and Mary Quarterly* 3, no. 4 (October 1946): 461–86.

Jackson, Helen H., and Valerie Sherer Mathes. *A Century of Dishonor: A Sketch of the United States Government's Dealings with Some of the Indian Tribes.* 1881; reprint, Norman: University of Oklahoma Press, 1995.

Jacobs, Wilbur R., ed. *The Paxton Riots and the Frontier Theory*. Chicago: Rand McNally, 1967.

Jenkins, Howard W. "Fragments of a Journal Kept by Samuel Foulke, of Bucks County, While a Member of the Colonial Assembly of Pennsylvania. 1762–3–4." *Pennsylvania Magazine of History and Biography* 5 (1881): 60–73.

Jennings, Francis. *Empire of Fortune: Crowns, Colonies and Tribes in the Seven Years War in America*. New York: Norton, 1988.

Kent, Barry C. *Susquehanna's Indians.* Harrisburg: Pennsylvania Historical and Museum Commission, 1984.

Klein, H.M.J., and William F. Diller. *The History of St. James' Church, 1744–1944.* Lancaster, PA: St. James' Vestry, 1944.

Klein, Randolph S. *Portrait of an Early American Family: The Shippens of Pennsylvania Across Five Generations*. Philadelphia: University of Pennsylvania Press, 1975.

Kozuskanich, Nathan. "Who Ever Proclaimed War with Part of a Nation, and Not with the Whole? The Paxton Riots and Perceptions of Civil Society in Pennsylvania." *Journal of Scotch-Irish Studies* 2, no. 1 (fall 2004): 61–63.

Labaree, Leonard W., and William B. Wilcox, eds. *The Papers of Benjamin Franklin.* New Haven, CT: Yale University Press, 1959.

Loskiel, George H. *History of the Mission of the United Brethren among the Indians in North America.* 1794; reprint, Whitefish, MT: Kessenger, 2003.

Martin, C.H. "Two Delaware Indians Who Lived on the Farm of Christian Hershey." *Papers of the Lancaster County Historical Society* 34 (1930): 217–20.

Merrell, James H. *Into the American Woods: Negotiators on the American Frontier.* New York: Norton, 1999.

Mombert, Jacob I. *An Authentic History of Lancaster County in the State of Pennsylvania.* Lancaster, PA: J.E. Barr, 1869.

Morgan, George H. *Annals of Harrisburg*. Harrisburg, PA: Geo. A. Brooks, 1858.

Myers, James P., Jr. "The Rev. Thomas Barton's Authorship of 'The Conduct of the Paxton Men, Impartially Represented' (1764)." *Pennsylvania History* 61, no. 2 (1994): 155–84.

———. "Thomas Barton's 'Unanimity and Public Spirit' (1755) Controversy and Plagiarism on the Pennsylvania Frontier." *Pennsylvania Magazine of History and Biography* 119, no. 3 (1995): 225–48.

Parkman, Francis. *The Conspiracy of Pontiac and the Indian War after the Conquest of Canada*. Vol. 2. Boston: Little, Brown, 1898.

Perry, William S. *Historical Collections Relating to the American Colonial Church*. Vol. 2: Pennsylvania. 1871; reprint, New York: AMS Press, 1969.

Proud, Robert. *The History of Pennsylvania in North America*. Vol. 2. Philadelphia: Zachariah Poulson Jr., 1798.

"Report of the Committee to Place and Unveil a Marker Designating and Commemorating the Indian Town of Conestoga, in Manor Township, Lancaster County, Pennsylvania." *Papers of the Lancaster County Historical Society* 28, no. 9 (1924): 129–52.

Richter, Daniel K. *Facing East from Indian Country*. Cambridge, MA: Harvard University Press, 2001.

Rowe, Gail S. *Embattled Bench*. Newark: University of Delaware Press, 1994.

Rupp, I. Daniel. *History of Lancaster County*. Lancaster, PA: Gilbert Hills, 1844.

Russell, Marvin F. "Thomas Barton and Pennsylvania's Colonial Frontier." *Pennsylvania History* 46, no. 4 (1979): 313–34.

Schock, Edwin Thomas, Jr. "The 'Cloven Foot' Rediscovered: The Historiography of the Conestoga Massacre through Three Centuries of Scholarship." *Journal of the Lancaster County Historical Society* 96, no. 3 (Fall 1994): 99–112.

Silver, Peter. *Our Savage Neighbors: How Indian War Transformed Early America*. New York: Norton, 2008.

Slaughter, Thomas P. "Interpersonal Violence in a Rural Setting: Lancaster County in the Eighteenth Century." *Pennsylvania History* 58, no. 2 (April 1971): 98–123.

Stroh, Oscar H. *The Paxton Rangers and Some Facts about Pontiac's Rebellion*. Harrisburg, PA: self-published, 1982.

Vaughan, Alden T. "Frontier Banditti and the Indians: The Paxton Boys' Legacy, 1763–1775." *Pennsylvania History* 51, no. 1 (1984): 1–29.

———. "Philadelphia Under Siege." *American History* 33, no. 6 (February 1999): 26–32.

Wallace, Benjamin. "The Insurrection of the Paxton Boys." *Presbyterian Quarterly Review* 13 (1860): 627–77.

Wallace, Paul A.W. *Indians in Pennsylvania*. Harrisburg: Pennsylvania Historical and Museum Commission, 1961.

Wood, Jerome H., Jr. *Conestoga Crossroads: Lancaster, Pennsylvania, 1730–1790*. Harrisburg: Pennsylvania Historical and Museum Commission, 1979.

Index

A

affidavits against the Conestogas 53, 55, 95, 168, 170
Agnew, Patrick 54
Allen, William 131, 138
Anabaptists 163, 164
Anglicans 142
Apology of the Paxton Volunteers 53, 55, 95, 168, 170, 173
archaeological excavations 156, 162
Armstrong, John 27, 42, 43, 47, 119, 120
Armstrong, Robert 55
Arnold, Benedict 93
Atlee, William Augustus 35, 145

B

Barber, Rhoda 83, 84, 85
Barber, Robert, Jr. 23, 24, 83
Barton, Thomas 34
  at Conestoga Indian Town 140, 141, 144
  background of 142, 143
  Conduct of the Paxton-Men and 53, 70, 75, 76, 77, 141, 143, 174
  death of 145
  delayed Christmas service and 143, 144
  during Revolution 145
  Edward Shippen and 140, 141, 174
  on Conestoga massacre 174
  plagiarism by 144
  reputation of 146
  stance on Indians of 142, 174
Baughman, Michael 130
Beck, Herbert 162
Bell, Thomas 121
Bickham, James 33, 35, 53
Boude, Samuel 35
Bouquet, Henry 126
Bow, Robert 131
Boyd, William 121
Brown, William 119
Burd, James 44

C

Calloway, Colin 107
Camenzind, Krista 106
Carpenter, Emanuel 52
Cartlidge, Edmond 157, 158
Cartlidge, John 157, 158
cartoons, with Paxton pamphlets 67
Cavaioli, Frank 102
Chrisly (Conestoga boy) 20, 23, 24, 28, 30, 170
Clayton, Asher 43, 117
Colden, Cadwalader 44
Conduct of the Paxton-Men (Barton) 53, 70, 75, 76, 77, 141, 143, 174
Conestoga Indians
  allegations against 48, 53, 54, 55, 95
  Benjamin Franklin and 69, 71, 72, 75
  burial of 152, 153, 155
  coroner's inquisition and 23
  customs of 20
  decline of 159
  descendants of 160
  Edward Shippen and 27, 41, 44, 61, 62, 139
  ghosts of 152
  in Lancaster workhouse 27, 29, 30, 31, 33
  Iroquois and 57, 173
  John Elder and 64, 133
  John Hay and 64
  John Penn and 27, 44, 50, 51, 52, 137
  magistrates and 52, 136
  massacre of 21, 36, 37, 71, 82, 83, 84, 85, 89, 90, 91
  memorials to 150, 152, 156, 161, 162
  names of 20, 29
  neighbors of 19, 23, 130
  petition for relief of 20
  removal plans for 26, 30, 33, 159
  Thomas Barton and 76, 141, 143
  treaties with 20, 30, 157
  William Penn and 19
Conestoga Indian Town 19, 21, 24, 130, 155, 156, 157, 159
Conestoga Manor 129
Conyngham, Redmond 170
  background of 87
  Lancaster Intelligencer series and 88, 89, 90, 92, 93, 94, 95, 97, 98, 99, 100, 101, 102, 105, 108, 120
  motivations of 93
  Provincial Correspondence and 87
Cowden, Matthew 95
Crowley, James 171
Cummings, Hubertis M. 101
Cunningham, Charles 55

D

Day, Sherman 88
De Haas, J.P. 120, 172
Derry Presbyterian Church 171
Derry Township 17, 37, 130, 167
Dickey, Moses 95, 96
Donegal Presbyterian Church 33, 114, 129, 175
Donegal Township 17, 33, 37, 129, 130, 167, 171
Donnally, Felix 33, 38, 42, 62, 91, 135, 136, 152
Dove, David James 68, 69
Dowd, Gregory 106
Dunbar, John Raine 100

E

Egle, William Henry 116
  affidavits against Conestogas by 95, 96
  as acolyte of Redmond Conyngham 94, 95
  identification of Paxton Rangers by 121, 122
Elder, John 26, 42, 45, 53, 89, 91, 101, 170
  as instigator of massacre 119, 133, 134
  as minister 116, 127
  as Paxton Rangers' commander 115, 116, 117, 127
  Edward Shippen and 27, 139
  Harrisburg home of 172

landholdings of 134
letters on massacre by 27, 64, 118
not commissioned 172
stance on Indians of 129, 133
English
as Paxton Boys 45
as settlers 126
Ewing, John 168, 169

F

Fisher, Thomas 131
Forster, James 117
Forster, Thomas 27, 53, 55, 64, 95, 96, 116, 118
Foulke, Samuel 42, 136
Franklin, Benjamin 46, 47, 50, 67
Narrative of the Late Massacres and 69, 72, 73, 76, 79, 92, 129
Franz, George 89, 91, 102, 114, 127
French and Indian War 20, 25, 116, 127, 157
Fulton Opera House 149, 151, 152, 175
Fulton, Robert, Jr. 35
Fulton, Robert, Sr. 32, 45

G

Gage, Thomas 51, 57
Galloway, Joseph 65
Germans
as Paxton Boys 45
as settlers 34, 56, 126, 127, 129, 130
Germantown 47, 48
Gibson, James 47, 49, 119
Gnadenhutten, massacre at 57, 58
Goehring, Reaves 170
Gordon, Thomas 83
Gorrecht, William 152
Gray Wolf 165
Green, Timothy 117

H

Halifax, Lord 51
Hambright, John 53, 54
Hamilton, James 117, 127, 138, 139
Hanna, Charles 88, 171
Hanover Township 37
Harris, Alexander 98, 159
Harris, John, Jr. 26, 53, 93, 116, 118
landholdings of 134
stance on Indians of 134
Harris's Ferry 17, 37, 167
Hay, John 23, 28, 30, 33, 38, 41, 64, 92, 135, 173
Hazard's Register 83, 88, 169
Heckewelder, John 57, 81
Henderson, David 65, 66, 135
Henry, William, Jr. 81, 82, 83
Henry, William, Sr. 32, 35
Hershey, Christian 159
Hindle, Brooke 99, 100
Hoover, Lloyd 165
Hunt, Isaac 69
Hunter, William 87, 88, 163
Hyhotah 108

I

Improved Order of Red Men 152
Iroquois 56, 57, 140, 157, 164

J

Jackson, Helen Hunt 71, 99
Jacobs, Wilbur 101
Jennings, Francis 103, 104
Johnson, William 44, 56, 130, 140, 141, 172, 173, 174

K

Kendall, Benjamin 45
Kenny, Kevin 107, 108
Kent, Barry 155, 157, 158, 160
Kornhauser, Barry 151, 152
Kreider, Noah, Jr. 159
Kuhn, Adam Simon 28, 32, 35

L

Lancaster Borough 20, 31, 45
Lancaster County 17, 88, 165

Lancaster County Courthouse 31, 38, 39
Lancaster Intelligencer & Journal 87, 88, 149, 170
Lancaster Moravian Church 149
Lancaster workhouse 27, 28, 31, 42, 62, 175
land greed 128, 129, 130, 131, 160
Landis, David Herr 161, 162
Lenape Indians 26, 44, 56, 57, 127
LeRoy, Marie 54, 97
Likens, John 117
Lincoln, Charles 100
Logan, James 129, 130, 157, 158
Loose, John W.W. 126, 152
Loskiel, Charles Henry 80
Ludwig, Jacob 117

M

Manor Township 19, 122, 157, 158
Marafioti, Jessie 108, 109
Mary (Conestoga Indian) 159, 160
Mason, Charles 80, 136
McKee, Thomas 23, 61
Meloon, Richard 131
Mennonites
  as neighbors of Conestogas 20, 130
  as reconciliators with Indians 164, 165
  as settlers 54, 130, 163
Merrell, James 103, 104, 105
Merritt, Jane 106
Michael (Conestoga Indian) 159, 160
Mombert, Jacob 98, 136
Moore, Thomas 54
Moravian Indians 26, 34, 42, 44, 45, 48, 49, 52, 57, 73, 75
Morgan, George 98
Muhlenberg, Henry Melchior 42, 119
Myers, James P., Jr. 141, 143, 144, 174
My Lai, massacre at 125

N

Narrative of the Late Massacres (Franklin) 69, 71, 72, 73, 76, 79, 92, 129
Newcomer, Abraham 54
Nissly's Cemetery 42, 152
Norris, Isaac 135

P

Parkman, Francis 98, 99, 122
Parthemore, Frederick 122
Paxton Boys 51, 52, 56, 67, 118, 137, 167, 174
  characterizations of 47, 100, 101, 103, 104, 105, 106, 107, 115
  Declaration and Remonstrance of 48, 49, 128
  march on Philadelphia of 45, 47, 49
  naming of 45
Paxton pamphlets 53, 77, 100
Paxton Presbyterian Church 26, 96, 114, 115, 116, 133
Paxton Rangers 17, 25, 33, 37, 44, 74, 133
  characterizations of 79, 80, 83, 87, 92, 93, 94, 95, 97, 98, 99, 101
  identities of 102, 114, 115, 116, 119, 120, 121, 122
  massacre at Conestoga by 21
  massacre at Lancaster by 41, 42
  motivations of 125, 129, 130, 131
Paxton Town 17, 25, 56, 125, 127, 130, 134
Paxton Township 17, 102, 130, 167
Pemberton, Israel 114
Pemberton, James 136
Penn, John 26, 29, 42, 44, 51, 159
  assembly and 49, 113, 121, 137
  in defense of Philadelphia 45
  instructs magistrates 27, 43, 52, 55
  letters to 41, 62, 64, 91, 131
  massacre repercussions and 56
  meets with Paxton Boys 49
  Pennsylvania Assembly and 33
  proclamations against Paxton Rangers of 34, 44, 61
  Stump affair and 137
Penn, Thomas 129, 141

Penn, William 19, 20, 30, 51, 105, 106, 107, 157
Pennsylvania Assembly 27, 29, 33, 46, 49, 106, 113, 121, 137
Pennsylvania Provincial Council 42, 45, 52
Pennsylvania Supreme Court 55, 56
Peters, Richard 129
Peters, William 57
Philadelphia 25, 33, 42, 45, 46, 47
Poke, Robert 131
Pontiac's Rebellion 25, 56, 103, 117, 125, 127, 139, 142, 172
Presbyterians 35, 67, 69, 114, 126, 127
Proclamation of 1763 173
Proud, Robert 80, 81, 119, 136
Pynchon, Thomas 169

Q

Quakers 67, 69
  as critics of massacre 135, 137
  as Indian defenders 77, 79, 129
  as neighbors of Conestogas 20, 23, 75, 162
  in Philadelphia 42, 45, 46, 49, 52, 56

R

racism 72, 98, 103, 104, 105, 106, 107, 129
reconciliation conference 163, 164
Reed, John 121
religious hatred 23, 72, 76, 119, 127, 133, 139
Reynolds, John 136
Richards, Janet Keller 164
Richter, Conrad 171
Richter, Daniel 103, 105, 106, 163, 172
Rittenhouse, David 47, 142
Robertson, James 33, 44, 63, 83, 85, 92, 93, 100, 135, 136, 139
Ross, George 35, 145
Rostraver, Simon 122
Royal Scottish Highlanders 33, 44, 63, 83, 100, 106, 136, 139
Rupp, I. Daniel 97, 116

S

Sally (Conestoga woman) 20, 71
Sanders, Isaac 52
Sawantaeny 157
scalp bounty 49, 143, 168
Scots-Irish 116, 126
  appropriation of land by 129, 130
  as deponents against Conestogas 53
  as members of Paxton Presbyterian Church 114
  as Paxton Boys 45, 67
  as Paxton Rangers 17
  at Paxton 127
Seneca Indians 20, 160
Sheehays 20, 21, 30, 55
Shelley, Leo 143, 170
Shippen, Edward, III 23
  account of massacre by 62
  as Presbyterian 139
  at St. James Episcopal Church 35
  Conestoga Indians and 139
  death of 145
  family background of 173
  in Philadelphia 138
  letters to John Elder by 27, 62
  letters to Joseph Shippen by 28, 62
  letter to John Penn by 61
  magistrates and 28, 33, 43, 52
  marriage of 138
  Paxton Rangers and 33, 44, 137, 139
  political offices of 138
  reputation of 146
  slave ownership by 174
  stance on Indians of 138, 139
  Thomas Barton and 140, 141
Shippen, Edward, IV 138
Shippen, Joseph 28, 138
Shippen, Peggy 93
Shoemaker, Henry W. 122
Silver, Peter 107
Slaughter, Thomas 104
Slough, Matthias 23, 33, 38, 135
Smith, Matthew 47, 49, 89, 90, 96, 119

Society for the Propagation of the Gospel 141, 142, 174
Sock, George 20, 29, 55
Sock, Molly 30
Sock, Will 30, 37, 105, 122
allegations against 54, 65, 95, 97
background of 29
death of 39, 82
squatters 129, 131, 140
Stainton, Leslie 175
Stephens, Alexander 55, 168
Stewart, Charles 117
Stewart, Lazarus 89, 90, 93, 120, 121, 172
St. James Episcopal Church 34, 135, 142, 143, 145
Strong Wolf, Joseph 161, 162
Stump, Frederick 137
Susquehannock Indians 157, 159, 161, 163
descendants of 160
vocabulary of 29
Sutliff, Robert 81

T

Thompson, Mrs. 55
Thompson, Robert 28, 53
treaties 30, 49, 57, 81, 129, 157, 158
Trump, Larry 151, 152

V

Vaughan, Alden 103, 104

W

Wallace, Benjamin 93, 94
Wallace, Paul 100
Weiser, Conrad 159
Whisler, Jacob 130, 131, 140
White Swan Tavern 33, 38, 61
Wimer, James 85
Witthoft, John 175
Wix, Ron 114, 115
Wright, James 52, 113
Wright, Susanna 114, 169
Wright, Thomas 23, 52
Wright's Ferry 17, 23, 167

About the Author

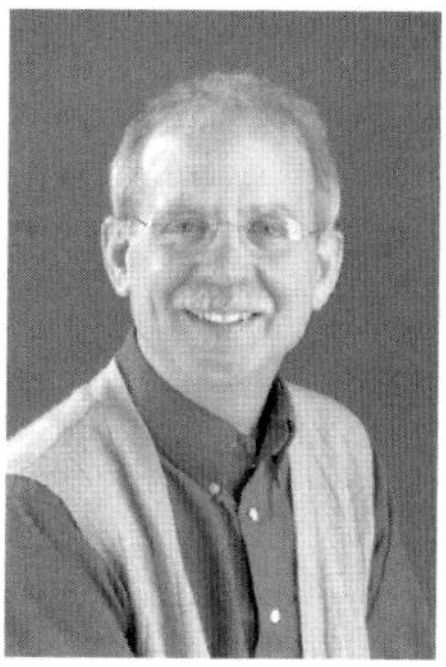

Photo by *Richard Hertzler.*

Jack Brubaker is a columnist and investigative reporter for Lancaster Newspapers. He has written six historical books, including *Remembering Lancaster County*, published by The History Press earlier this year. He lives with his wife, Christine, in Lancaster County's Manor Township, not far from where the Paxton Boys massacred the Conestoga Indians nearly 250 years ago.